SECRET CODES 2001

PlayStation® 2

PlayStation®

Dreamcast®

Nintendo 64®

Game Boy®

////IIBRADYGAMES

TAKE YOUR GAME FURTHER™

SECRET CODES 2001

©2001 Macmillan USA, Inc.

LEGAL STUFF

Brady Publishing
An Imprint of
Macmillan USA, Inc.
201 W. 103rd St.
Indianapolis, IN 46290

ISBN: 0-7440-0044-0
Library of Congress No.: 00-135438

Printing Code: The rightmost double-digit number is the year of the book's printing; the rightmost single-digit number is the number of the book's printing. For example, 00-1 shows that the first printing of the book occurred in 2000.

03 02 01 00   4 3 2 1

BRADYGAMES STAFF

Editor-In-Chief
H. Leigh Davis

Licensing Manager
David Waybright

Licensing Assistant
Mike Degler

Creative Director
Robin Lasek

Marketing Manager
Janet Eshenour

Marketing Assistant
Tricia Reynolds

CREDITS

Project Editor
Ken Schmidt

Screenshot Editor
Michael Owen

Book Designer
Dan Caparo

Production Designers
Lisa England
Bob Klunder
Jane Washburne
Tracy Wehmeyer

TABLE OF CONTENTS

PlayStation 2 Codes	4
PlayStation Codes	16
Dreamcast Codes	94
Nintendo 64 Codes	130
Game Boy Codes	196

GAME NAME	PAGE
DYNASTY WARRIORS 2	4
MIDNIGHT CLUB: STREET RACING	5
READY 2 RUMBLE BOXING ROUND 2	5
SSX	6
STREET FIGHTER EX3	8
SUMMONER	10
SWING AWAY GOLF	10
TEKKEN TAG TOURNAMENT	11
TIME SPLITTERS	12
UNREAL TOURNAMENT	14
X SQUAD	15

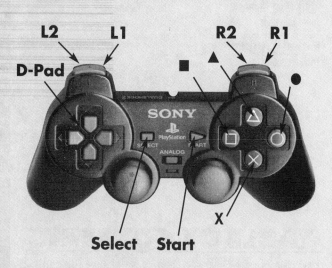

L2 L1 R2 R1

D-Pad ■ ▲ ●

X

Select Start

DYNASTY WARRIORS 2

ALL CHARACTERS

At the Title screen press ■, R1, ■, R2, ■, R2, ■, R1.

4

MIDNIGHT CLUB: STREET RACING

BAJA BUGGY

If you have a save game from Smuggler's Run, you can access the Baja Buggy in Arcade mode.

READY 2 RUMBLE BOXING ROUND 2

HAPPY HOLIDAYS!

On each Holiday (New Years, Valentines Day, Easter, July 4th, Halloween, Christmas) the game does a holiday theme, based on the internal clock. For example, on Halloween the ring turns orange and black and J.R. Flurry wears a skeleton costume. Change your clock and you can see all the Holiday themes!

CODES

EFFECT	CODE
Big Gloves mode	← → ↑ ↓, R1, R2
Chubby mode	→ → ↑ ↓ →, R1, R1, R2
Toothpick mode	→ → ↑ ↓ →, R1, R2
Zombie mode	← ↑ → ↓, R1, R1, R2

RUMBLING RING

Select Afro Thunder. Before the fight begins, press X, ■, X, X, ●, ▲ and the screen will shake!

CHAMPIONSHIP OUTFITS

Finish the game once in Championship Mode.

UNLOCK SECRET CHARACTERS

Beat Arcade Mode to unlock these secret characters in the following order:

Freak E. Deke	Freedom Brock
Michael Jackson	Rocket Samchay
G.C. Thunder	Mr. President
Wild "Stubby" Corley	The First Lady
Shaquille O'Neal	

Defeat Arcade Mode on the Hardest difficulty to open Rumbleman.

RUN WITH YOUR BOARD

At the Options Menu, hold R1 + L1 + R2 + L2 and press ■, ▲, ▲, X, ■, ▲, ●, X. Start a race and you will run with your board on your back. Repeat code to turn the cheat off.

ALL HINTS

At the Options Menu, hold R1 + L1 + R2 + L2 and press ●, X, ●, X, ●, X, ●, X. Start a race and while loading, it will run through all of the hints. This does take some time. Repeat the code at the Options Menu to turn off.

MAX STATS

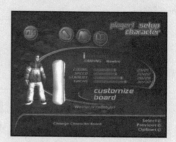

At the Options Menu, hold R1 + L1 + R2 + L2 and press X, X, X, X, X, X, X, ■. Re-enter to change the stats back.

ALL CHARACTERS, BOARDS, COURSES AND COSTUMES

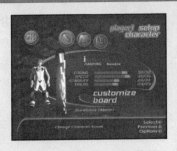

At the Options Menu, hold R1 + L1 + R2 + L2 and press Down, Left, Up, Right, X, ●, ▲, ■. Re-enter the code to disable the code and try to earn everything the fun way.

ALTERNATE UNLOCK CHARACTERS

Just start a game and earn gold medals to get the other characters:

NUMBER OF GOLDS	OPENS THIS CHARACTER
1	Jurgen
2	JP
3	ZOE
4	Hiro

UNLOCK ALTERNATE BOARDS

You start with 2 boards. Reach the following ranks to unlock each board.

RANK	BOARD
Rookie	3
Sensei	4
Contender	5
Natural	6
Star	7
Veteran	8
Champ	9
Superstar	10
Master	11

EARN ALTERNATE COSTUMES

The Trick Book is broken up into three difficulties: green circle, blue square and black diamond. Perform each of the green circle to get the third costume and the blue square to get the fourth costume.

UNLOCK ALTERNATE COURSES

To unlock the different race and showoff courses, just get a medal in the previous one.

UNLOCK "UNTRACKED" COURSE

Earn a Gold medal on Pipe Dream and Aloha Jam.

STREET FIGHTER EX3
HIDDEN CHARACTERS

After you clear Original Mode, you will unlock hidden characters that will appear on the character select screen. The characters will appear in this order: Sagat, Bison, Garuda, Shadow Geist, Kairi, Pullum, Area, Darun, and Vulcano.

You can unlock all nine of these characters as you continue to clear the game, regardless of the number of continues or difficulty level, but you can only unlock one hidden character for each character that clears the game. In other words, if you clear the game nine times with Ryu, you will only have unlocked one hidden character.

THE MEDALLION SYSTEM

In Original Mode, you can collect Medals by completing the tasks assigned to you before the Round begins.

If you collect all the medals of a certain color, you can get the following bonuses.

ALL BRONZE MEDALS

Narration by Sakura. The voice you hear before each Round starts will become Sakura's voice.

On the Character Select screen, put the cursor on Sakura and push the select button.

ALL SILVER MEDALS

"Bison II" becomes playable, but only in Original Mode.

On the Character Select screen, put the cursor on Bison and hold Select while choosing him. If you

chose Bison II as your main character, you can't get any other characters on your team.

ALL GOLD MEDALS

Evil Ryu becomes playable.

On the Character Select screen, put the cursor on Ryu and hold Select while choosing him.

When fighting with multiple players (i.e. tag mode or team battle), if somebody picks Ryu on a team, they cannot pick Evil Ryu on the same team as well.

ALL PLATINUM MEDALS

Opens up new modes: "vs Bison II" and "vs True Bison". In these modes you can battle with Bison II or True Bison immediately.

Select "vs Bison II" or "vs True Bison" from the Arena Mode menu.

MEDALLION SUBSTITUTES

If you're having a hard time collecting all of the medals, you can meet the conditions below to open the same secrets.

Clear Original Mode eight times using Sakura instead of getting all Bronze Medals.

Clear Original Mode eight times using Bison instead of getting all Silver Medals.

Clear Original Mode eight times using Ryu instead of getting all Gold Medals.

Defeat Bison II in "vs Bison II" and True Bison "vs True Bison" mode four times each instead of getting all Platinum Medals.

CUT-IN CHARACTERS

If the following conditions are met during play in Original Mode, hidden characters will interrupt your battle. If you finish every stage with a Meteor Combo, Meteor Tag Combo, or Critical Parade:

If you're playing as Hokuto or Nanase, Kairi will cut in.

If you're playing as Skullomania or Sharon, Shadow Geist will cut in.

If you're playing as Sagat, Ken, Sakura, or Bison/Bison II, Evil Ryu will cut in.

HOW TO FIGHT BISON II

If you meet all of the conditions listed below, Bison II will appear in the Final Stage.

NORMAL DIFFICULTY:

❖ Continue winning with a Finish Combo (see note)

❖ Your Score is over 500,000 points

❖ Use no continues

> **NOTE**
>
> A Finish Combo indicates finishing off your opponent with two characters at the same time. However, since you have no teammates in Stage 1, finishing with a Meteor Combo is treated the same as finishing with a Meteor Tag Combo or a Critical Parade.

HARD DIFFICULTY:

❖ Use no continues

SUMMONER

EXTRA MOVIE

Select Credits and after they scroll through a bonus movie will start. You can press X to skip the credits and go straight to the movie.

SWING AWAY GOLF

OPEN ALL GOLFERS

At the Main Menu press L2, R2, L2, R2, Up, Right, Down, Left, L1, R1. You will hear a sound if entered correctly.

TEKKEN TAG TOURNAMENT

EXTRA CHARACTERS

As you finish the game with each character you open the following:

- ❖ Kunimitsu
- ❖ Bruce Irvin
- ❖ Jack-2
- ❖ Lee Chaolan
- ❖ Wang Jinrey
- ❖ Roger & Alex
- ❖ Kuma & Panda
- ❖ Kazuya Mishima
- ❖ Ogre
- ❖ True Ogre
- ❖ Prototype Jack
- ❖ Mokujin & Tetsujin
- ❖ Devil and Angel
- ❖ Unknown

STAGE SELECT IN PRACTICE MODE

Highlight Practice Mode, hold L2 and press R2 1 to 20 times to get stages 1-20.

TIGER

At the character select screen, highlight Eddy and press Start.

ANGEL

After unlocking Devil, highlight Devil at the character select and press Start.

HEIHACHI

Complete Arcade mode in less than 5 minutes 30 seconds with no loses

THEATRE MODE

Defeat arcade mode once.

GALLERY MODE

Unlock Devil

TEKKEN BOWL MODE

Unlock Ogre.

JUKEBOX IN TEKKEN BOWL

Get 200 Points in Tekken Bowl.

DR. B

Earn the high score in Tekken Bowl.

A B C D E F G H I J K L M N O P Q R S T U V W X Y Z

TIME SPLITTERS

STORY MODE

Defeating each level in Story Mode earns you new Playable Characters, Bots in Arcade Mode, new Arcade Levels and various cheats. The following table lists what you get for beating each level of Story Mode for each difficulty.

LEVEL	EASY	NORMAL	HARD
1935 Tomb	Cultist Character	Graveyard Level	Eyes Mummy Character
1970 Chinese	Chinese Chef Character	Site Level	Suit Hoodlum Character
2005 Cyberden	Badass Cyborg Character; Village, Chemical Plant, Planet-X Levels; New Arcade Bot	Streets Level	Female Cyborg Character
1950 Village	Period Horror Bot Set; New Arcade Bot	Castle Level	Fishwife Mutant Character
1985 Chemical Plant	Usual Suspects Bot Set; New Arcade Bot	Bank Level	Lumberjack Character
2020 Planet-X	Space Opera Bot Set; R108 and Gretel Characters; Mansion, Docks, Spaceways Levels; New Arcade Bot	Spaceship Level	Pillar Alien Character; Headless Characters cheat

2000 Docks	Law and Order Bot Set; New Arcade Bot	Compound Level	Gasmask Soldier Character
2035 Spaceways	Challenge Mode	Warzone Level	Spaceways Stewardess Character and Bot

CHALLENGE MODE

Defeating each challenge in Challenge Mode earns you new Playable Characters, Bots in Arcade Mode and various cheats. The following Table lists what you get for beating each Challenge.

DEFEAT CHALLENGE	TO GET
1-A	Zombies Bot Set
1-B	Green & Brown Zombie Characters
1-C	Police, Skull, & Jacket Zombie Characters
2-A	Duckman Bot
2-B	All enemies are Ducks
2-C	Duckman Drake Character
3-A	Robofish Bot
3-B	All enemies are Robofish
3-C	Robofish Character
4-A	Nothing
4-B	Enemy Bricks Cheat
4-C	Brick Weapon in Arcade Mode
5-A	Impersonator Bot

DEFEAT CHALLENGE	TO GET
5-B	All enemies are Impersonators
5-C	The Impersonator Character
6-A	Nothing
6-B	Gasmask SWAT Character
6-C	Veiled SWAT Character
7-A	Gingerbread Man Bot
7-B	All enemies are Gingerbread Men
7-C	Gingerbread Man Character
8-A	Farrah Fun Bunny Bot
8-B	All enemies are Bunnies
8-C	Farrah Fun Bunny Character
9-A	TimeSplitters Bot
9-B	TimeSplitter 1 Character
9-C	TimeSplitter 2 Character

UNREAL TOURNAMENT

CURRENT MAP ADVANCE

Hit PAUSE and press ↑ ↓ ← → →
← ●.

Gives you an immediate victory in the current level

LEVEL LADDER

On the resume game menu, select an existing saved game, and press
↑ ↓ ↑ ↑ ← ↑ → ↓.

Immediately completes all missions and opens all levels

GOD MODE

While PAUSED, press ■ ● ← →
● ■.

ALL AMMO

While PAUSED, press ← → ● ●
● → ←.

UNLOCK BIG HEAD MUTATOR

In the main menu press ← → ←
→ ← → ● ● ●.

UNLOCK FATBOY

In the main menu press ● ● ●
↑ ↓ ↓ ↑ ● ● ●.

The more frags you get, the fatter you get. The more you are fragged, the thinner you get.

UNLOCK STEALTH

In the main menu press ■ ■ ●
● ■ ■ ● ●.

X SQUAD

PRIVATE RANK

At the main menu, press ■, ●, ▲. You will start the game with Michaels 9mmS with 99 ammo.

SERGEANT RANK

At the main menu, press ▲, ●, ■, then start a new game. You will start the game with no weight limit, Taylor M82, Michaels 9mmS with 99 ammo.

CAPTAIN RANK

At the main menu, press ●, R1, ●, L1, ▲, R2. You will start the game with radar, no weight limit, Taylor M82, Michaels 9mmS with 99 ammo.

MAJOR RANK

At the main menu, press L2, ■, R2, ▲, L1, ●, R1. You will start the game with level 3 shield, Level 3 sensor, radar, no weight limit, Taylor M82, Michaels 9mmS with 99 ammo.

LIEUTENANT RANK

At the main menu, press R1, L2, L1, R2. You will start the game with level 2 shield, no weight limit, Taylor M82, Michaels 9mmS with 99 ammo.

COLONEL RANK

At the main menu, press ▲, ■, ●, ■, ▲, ●. You will start the game with level 3 shield, level 3 sensor, radar, no weight limit, beginner level of all weapons with 99 ammo.

GENERAL RANK

At the main menu, press L1, L1, L2, L2, R1, R1, R2, R2. You will start the game with level 3 shield, level 3 sensor, radar, no weight limit, intermediate level of all weapons with 99 ammo.

MASTER OF X-SQUAD RANK

At the main menu, press ● (x4), ▲, ■ (x4). You will start the game with level 3 shield, level 3 sensor, radar, no weight limit, master level of all weapons with 99 ammo.

GAME NAME	PAGE
A BUG'S LIFE	19
ALIEN RESURRECTION	19
APE ESCAPE	20
ARMY MEN AIR ATTACK	20
ARMY MEN: SARGE'S HEROES	22
ARMY MEN: SARGE'S HEROES 2	22
BLADE	23
BUGS BUNNY: LOST IN TIME	23
CENTIPEDE	24
CLOCK TOWER 2: THE STRUGGLE WITHIN	24
COLIN MCRAE RALLY	25
COOL BOARDERS 4	28
CROC 2	28
CTR (CRASH TEAM RACING)	29
CYBERTIGER	31
DAVE MIRRA FREESTYLE BMX	32
DESTRUCTION DERBY RAW	33
DRIVER	35
DUKE NUKEM LAND OF THE BABES	37
FEAR EFFECT	39
FIGHTING FORCE 2	39
GRAND THEFT AUTO 2	40
HOT WHEELS TURBO RACING	41
JARRETT & LABONTE RACING	43
KNOCKOUT KINGS 2000	43
KURT WARNER'S ARENA FOOTBALL UNLEASHED	45
LEGO ROCK RAIDERS	47
MADDEN NFL 2000	48
MEDAL OF HONOR: UNDERGROUND	50
MEDIEVIL II	50
MTV SPORTS: SKATEBOARDING	51
MUPPET: RACE MANIA	51
NASCAR 2000	52
NASCAR RUMBLE	53
NBA LIVE 2000	53

GAME NAME	PAGE
NBA SHOWTIME	55
NCAA FOOTBALL 2000	59
NCAA GAMEBREAKER 2001	63
NFL BLITZ 2001	64
NFL GAMEDAY 2001	67
NO FEAR DOWNHILL MOUNTAIN BIKE RACING	70
POWER RANGERS: LIGHTSPEED RESCUE	70
PRO PINBALL BIG RACE USA	70
QUAKE II	71
RAINBOW SIX	71
RAMPAGE THROUGH TIME	72
RC STUNT COPTER	73
ROLLCAGE STAGE 2	73
SLED STORM	74
SPACE INVADERS	76
SPIDER-MAN	76
STAR TREK: INVASION	77
STAR WARS DEMOLITION	77
STAR WARS EPISODE 1: THE PHANTOM MENACE	78
STREET SK8ER 2	78
SUPERCROSS 2000	79
SUPERCROSS CIRCUIT	81
SYPHON FILTER 2	81
TARZAN	82
TENCHU 2: BIRTH OF THE STEALTH ASSASSINS	83
TEST DRIVE 6	84
TEST DRIVE LE MANS	85
TOMB RAIDER CHRONICLES	87
TOMORROW NEVER DIES	87
TONY HAWK'S PRO SKATER 2	89
TRIPLE PLAY 2001	92
URBAN CHAOS	92
WCW MAYHEM	93
X-MEN: MUTANT ACADEMY	93

PLAYSTATION®
LEGEND

ABBREV.	WHAT IT MEANS
Left	Left on D-pad
Right	Right on D-pad
Down	Down on D-pad
Up	Up on D-pad
▲	▲ button
●	● button
X	X button
■	■ button
Start	Start button
Select	Select button
L1	L1 button
L2	L2 button
R1	R1 button
R2	R2 button

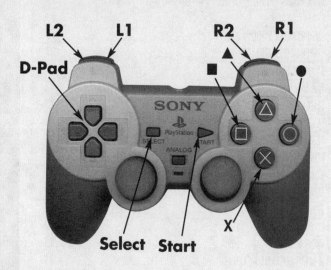

A BUG'S LIFE

EXTRA LIVES

Collect the letters for **FLIK** in the Training Level to gain a life. You can repeat this as often as you want.

Extra Lives.

ALIEN RESURRECTION

CHEAT MODE

At the main menu or Options menu, press Circle, Left, Right, Circle, Up, R2. This will add a Cheat Menu option to the Options menu.

RESEARCH MODE

At the main menu or Options menu, press Square, Up, Down, Circle, Left, R1. This will add a Research option to the Options menu.

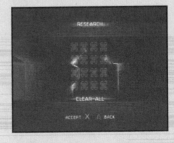

APE ESCAPE

COLLECT UP TO 99 EXPLOSIVE BULLETS
Pause the game and press R2, Down, L2, Up, Right, Down, Right, Left.

ARMY MEN AIR ATTACK

ALL CO-PILOTS
Enter the following as a password:
Up, Down, Up, Down, Up, Down, Up, Down.

All Co-Pilots.

ONE-PLAYER PASSWORDS

MISSION	PASSWORD
2	X, Down, Left, Left, ■, ●, ●, Right
3	▲, Up, Left, Right, Down, ▲, ■, Up
4	Down, Down, ■, ■, Left, Right, ●, X
5	Right, Right, X, ●, Down, Up, Down, Up
6	■, ●, X, ■, [TR], Left, Up, Right
7	■, ●, X, ■, ▲, Left, Up, Right

Mission 7 Password.

8	Right, Down, Left, Up, ▲, Down, Up, Down
9	●, ●, Right, Up, Right, Up, X, X
10	X, Down (X4), X, Left, Right
11	▲, Up, ●, Down, ■, Left, X, Right
12	Up, Up, ▲, ▲, Left, Left, ●, ●
13	Left, Down, Left, Down, ■, ●, ■, ●
14	Left, Left, Up, Right, Right, Up, Down, X
15	■, Right, Left, ●, ●, Up, Down, ■

TWO-PLAYER PASSWORDS

MISSION	PASSWORD
2	Right, Up, ■, X, Up, ●, Up, Right
3	Left, Down, Left, Down, Up (X4)
4	■, X, X, ■, ●, ▲, ▲, ■
5	●, ●, ■, Down, Down, ■, X, X
6	X, Up, ●, Down, ▲, Left, ■, Right
7	Up, Down (X3), Right, Left (X3)
8	Left, Left, ▲, Right, Right, ▲, Up, Up
9	■ (X3), ●, Down (X3), Left
10	●, Up, Left, ■, Up, Left, Down, Down
11	▲, ●, ▲, ●, Up, Up, Down, Down
12	Up, Down, Left, Right, ●, ●, Up, ■
13	X, Left (X3), ■, ▲, ●, X
14	Left, Down, Left, Down, ■, ●, ■, ●
15	Down (X4), X, X, ●, ●
16	▲, Down, ▲, Down, ■, Up, ■, Up

21

ARMY MEN: SARGE'S HEROES

ALL WEAPONS
Pause the game and press ■, ●, R1, L1.

ARMY MEN: SARGE'S HEROES 2

PASSWORDS

LEVEL	PASSWORD
Bridge	Fllngdwn
Fridge	Gtmlk
Freezer	Chllbb
Inside Wall	Clsngn
Graveyard	Dgths
Castle	Rnknstn
Tan Base	Bdbz
Revenge	Lbbck
Desk	Dskjb
Bed	Gtslp
Blue Town	Smllvll
Cashier	Chrgt
Train	Ntbrt
Rockets	Rdglr
Pool Table	Fstnls
Pinball Table	Whswzrd

TIN FOIL UNIFORM
Enter TNMN as a password.

LEVEL SELECT
Enter LLLVLS as a password.

ALL WEAPONS
Enter NSRLS as a password.

FULL AMMO
Enter MMLUSRM as a password.

MINI MODE

Enter DRVLLVSMM as a password.

DEBUG

Enter THDTST as a password.

TANK

Enter NRLTK as a password.

BLADE

INFINITE AMMO

At the Main Menu, press Down, Right, Up, Left, L2, L1, R2, R1. Then to open an in-game Cheat Menu, press Start during a game.

INFINITE LIFE

At the Main Menu, press Left (x3), Right, L2, L1, R2, R1. Then to open an in-game Cheat Menu, press Start during a game.

BUGS BUNNY: LOST IN TIME

LEVEL SELECT

At the Level Select screen, press and hold L2 + R1 and then press X, ■, R2, L1, ●, X, ■, ■, ■.

Level Select.

B C D E F G H I J K L M N O P Q R S T U V W X Y Z

CENTIPEDE

EXTRA LIVES

During an Adventure game, pause and press L1, L1, L2, L1. Unpause the game, pause it again, and then press Right.

Extra Lives.

INVINCIBILITY

Enter the Extra Lives cheat and add an odd number of lives. The word "Invulnerability" will appear when done correctly.

Invincibility.

LEVEL SELECT

Select Adventure and then at the Level Select screen press R1, R1, R2, R1. You will hear a sound when entered correctly.

Level Select.

CLOCK TOWER 2: THE STRUGGLE WITHIN

SPECIAL POWER CHARM

At the Title screen, hold L1 + R1 + L2 + R2 while starting a new game.

ALTERNATE OUTFIT

At the Title screen, hold L1 + R2 + Select + ▲ while starting a new game.

Alternate Outfit.

SOUND TEST

At the Title screen, press Left, ●, Down, ▲, Right, ■, Up, X, L1, R2, L2, R1 + Start. You'll find the Sound Test option at the Options screen.

Sound Test.

COLIN MCRAE RALLY

CHEAT CODES

Enter one of the following as your name. These codes only work in Rally or Time Trial mode.

CODE	EFFECT
DIDDYCARS	Small Cars
HOVERCRAFT	Hover Cars

Hover Cars.

CODE	EFFECT
BLANCMANGE	Green Jelly Car

Green Jelly Car.

CODE	EFFECT
TINFOILED	Metallic Cars
SHOEBOXES	All Cars
BACKSEAT	Nicky Grist Driver
SILKYSMOOTH	60 Frames Per Second
PEASOUPER	Fog

Fog.

CODE	EFFECT
BUTTONBASH	Power Accelerator
HELIUMNICK	Co-Driver with Squeaky Voice
WHITEBUNNY	Right-Side Driver

Right-Side Driver.

CODE	EFFECT
DIRECTORCUT	Replay Option
NIGHTRIDER	Night Races

Night Races.

SKCART	Mirror Tracks
OPENROADS	All Tracks

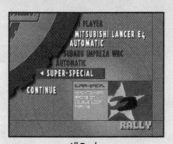

All Tracks.

KITCAR	Turbo boost (press Select)
MOONWALK	Low gravity
MOREOOMPH	Double engine power
FORKLIFT	Rear wheel steering
TROLLEY	4-wheel steering

COOL BOARDERS 4

ALL MOUNTAINS, CHARACTERS, AND BOARDS

In 1-player mode, enter **ICHEAT** as your name. You will hear someone say "Hey, no cheating" when entered correctly.

All Mountains, Characters, and Boards.

ALL SPECIAL EVENTS

In 1-player mode, enter **IMSPE-CIAL** as your name. You will hear someone say "Hey, no cheating" when entered correctly.

All Special Events.

CROC 2

CHEAT MODE

At the Title screen, press and hold L1 and press ▲, Left, Left, Right, ■, Up, Up, Left, ●. Then during gameplay, press L2 + R2.

Cheat Mode.

9999 CRYSTALS

At the Title screen, press and hold L1 and press ■, ■, ●, Down, Left, Right, Left, and Right. Then during gameplay, press and hold R2 and press ■ to add crystals.

9999 Crystals.

UNLIMITED LIVES

At the Title screen, press and hold L1 and press ●, Down, Left, Up, Right, ▲, and Down.

START WITH NINE HEARTPOTS

At the Title screen, press and hold R1 and press Left, Left, Down, ●, ■, and ■.

CTR (CRASH TEAM RACING)

RACE AS PENTA PENGUIN

At the Main Menu, press and hold L1 + R1 and press Down, Right, ▲, Down, Left, ▲, and Up. You will hear a sound when entered correctly. You can race as Penta Penguin in all modes except Adventure mode.

Race as Penta Penguin.

RACE AS KOMODO JOE

At the Main Menu, press and hold L1 + R1 and press Down, ●, Left, Left, ▲, Right, and Down. You will hear a sound when entered correctly. You can race as Komodo Joe in all modes except Adventure mode.

RACE AS DR. N. TROPHY

At the Main Menu, press and hold L1 + R1 and press Down, Left, Right, Up, Down, Right, and Right. You will hear a sound when entered correctly. You can race as Dr. N. Trophy in all modes except Adventure mode.

A B C D E F G H I J K L M N O P Q R S T U V W X Y Z

RACE AS PAPU PAPU

At the Main Menu, press and hold L1 + R1 and press Left, ▲, Right, Down, Right, ●, Left, Left, and Down. You will hear a sound when entered correctly. You can race as Papu Papu in all modes except Adventure mode.

RACE AS PINSTRIPE

At the Main Menu, press and hold L1 + R1 and press Left, Right, ▲, Down, Right, and Down. You will hear a sound when entered correctly. You can race as Pinstripe in all modes except Adventure mode.

Race as Pinstripe.

RACE AS RIPPER ROO

At the Main Menu, press and hold L1 + R1 and press Right, ●, ●, Down, Up, Down, and Right. You will hear a sound when entered correctly. You can race as Ripper Roo in all modes except Adventure mode.

INVISIBILITY

At the Main Menu, press and hold L1 + R1 and press Up, Up, Down, Right, Right, and Up. You will hear a sound when entered correctly.

Invisibility.

99 WUMPA FRUIT/ALWAYS JUICED

At the Main Menu, press and hold L1 + R1 and press Down, Right, Right, Down, and Down. You will hear a sound when entered correctly.

UNLIMITED MASKS

At the Main Menu, press and hold L1 + R1 and press Left, ▲,

Unlimited Masks.

Right, Left, ●, Right, Down, and Down. You will hear a sound when entered correctly.

SCRAPBOOK OPTION

At the Main Menu, press and hold L1 + R1 and press Up, Up, Down, Right, Right, Left, Right, ▲, and Right. You will hear a sound when entered correctly. In addition, a new option appears on the Main Menu called "Scrapbook."

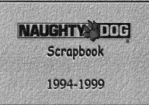

Scrapbook Option.

TURBO COUNTER

At the Main Menu, press and hold L1 + R1 and press ▲, Down, Down, ●, Up. You will hear a sound when entered correctly.

Turbo Counter.

SUPER TURBO PADS

At the Main Menu, press and hold L1 + R1 and press ▲, Right, Right, ●, and Left. You will hear a sound when entered correctly.

SPYRO: RIPTO'S RAGE DEMO

At the Main Menu, press and hold L1 + R1 and press Down, ●, ▲, and Right.

CYBERTIGER

COURSE PASSWORD

At the Course Select screen, press ● to access the Password screen. To access the courses, enter the following passwords:

COURSE	PASSWORD
Cyber Badlands	HARESO

Cyber Badlands.

Cyber Canyons	NAMOPI
Cyber Sawgrass	SECARE
Cyber Summerlin	PORASO
All Courses	POQAKI

All Courses.

DAVE MIRRA
FREESTYLE BMX

UNLOCK SLIM JIM

At the Rider Select screen, press Down, Down, Left, Right, Up, Up, Circle.

ALL BIKES

At the Bike Select screen, press Up, Left, Up, Down, Up, Right, Left, Right, Circle.

ALL STYLES

At the Style Select screen, press Left, Up, Right, Down, Left, Down, Right, Up, Left, Circle.

DESTRUCTION DERBY RAW

ACCESS THE HUMMER

At the Secret Code screen, enter **humall**.

DIE HARD TRILOGY 2

DEBUG MENU

At the Main Menu, press L1, L1, ●, ●, ■, ■ to access a movie player and level select.

3rd Person Action/Adventure Mode

INVINCIBILITY

During gameplay, pause the game and press ▲, ▲, ●, ●, L1, L2.

ALL WEAPONS

During gameplay, pause the game and press ■, ■, ●, ●, L1, L1.

INFINITE AMMO

During gameplay, pause the game and press L1, L1, R1, R1, ●, ●.

SLOW ROCKETS

During gameplay, pause the game and press L1, R1, R1, L1, ▲, ■.

DISABLE LASER SIGHTING

During gameplay, pause the game and press L1, L1, ▲, ▲, L1, L1.

HEADS POP OFF

During gameplay, pause the game and press ■, ■, ●, ●, R1, R1.

SKELETON

During gameplay, pause the game and press ●, ■, ▲, ▲, ■, ●.

GIVE ENEMIES BIG HEAD

During gameplay, pause the game and press R1, R1, L1, L1, ▲, ▲.

ELECTRIC

During gameplay, pause the game and press ■, ■, L1, L1, R1, R1.

1ST-PERSON VIEW

During gameplay, pause the game and press ●, ▲, ▲, ■.

DAMPEN CAMERA

During gameplay, pause the game and press ▲, ▲, ▲, ■, ■, ■.

Extreme Driving Mode

INVINCIBILITY

During gameplay, pause the game and press ▲, ▲, ●, ●, L1, L2.

UNLIMITED TIME

During gameplay, pause the game and press L1, R1, ■, ■, R1, L1.

UNLIMITED NITRO

During gameplay, pause the game and press L1, L1, R1, R1, ●, ●.

FASTER CAR

During gameplay, pause the game and press ●, ■, R1, R1, ●, L1.

ONLY WHEELS

During gameplay, pause the game and press L1, R1, R1, L1, L1, R1.

RAIN

During gameplay, pause the game and press ■, ■, L1, L1, ▲, ●.

Sharpshooter Mode

INVINCIBILITY

During gameplay, pause the game and press ▲, ▲, ●, ●, L1, L2.

UNLIMITED AMMO

During gameplay, pause the game and press L1, L1, R1, R1, ●, ●.

SLOW ROCKETS

During gameplay, pause the game and press L1, R1, R1, L1, ▲, ■.

ALL WEAPONS

During gameplay, pause the game and press ■, ■, ●, ●, L1, L1.

SLOW MOTION

During gameplay, pause the game and press ▲, L1, ▲, L1, ▲, L1.

AUTO RELOAD

During gameplay, pause the game and press ■, ■, ▲, ▲, ●, ●.

DRIVER

You must enter the following codes at the Main Menu, and then select the Cheats option and turn on the cheats:

Cheats Menu.

EFFECT	CODE
Invincibility	L2, L2, R2, R2, L2, R2, L2, L1, R2, R1, L2, L1, L1
Immunity	L1, L2, R1 (X4), L2, L2, R1, R1, L1, L1, R2
Rear Wheel Drive	R1, R1, R1, R2, L2, R1, R2, L2, L1, R2, R1, L2, L1
Stilts	R2, L2, R1, R2, L2, L1, R2, R2, L2, L2, L1, R2, R1

Stilts.

Mini Cars (Normal Collision)	R1, R2, R1, R2, L1, L2, R1, R2, L1, R1, L2, L2, L2

Mini Cars.

EFFECT	CODE
Antipodean (Upside Down)	R2, R2, R1, L2, L1, R2, L2, L1, R2, R2, L2, R2, L1

Upside Down.

Credits	L1, L2, R1, R2, L1, R1, R2, L2, R1, R2, L1, L2, R1

DUKE NUKEM LAND OF THE BABES

BIG HEAD DUKE

At the Cheat Menu, press Square, Square, X, Circle, Circle, X, Square.

TINY HEAD DUKE

At the Cheat Menu, press Square, X, Circle, Circle, X, Square, Square.

BIG HEAD ENEMIES

At the Cheat Menu, press X, X, R1, X, L1, X.

TINY HEAD ENEMIES

At the Cheat Menu, press X, L1, X, R1, X, X.

START WITH FULL EGO

At the Cheat Menu, press R1, R1, Circle, Circle, L1, L1, R2.

FIRST-PERSON CAMERA

At the Cheat Menu, press L2, R1, L1, R2, Circle, X, Square.

WACKY CINEMATICS

At the Cheat Menu, press L1, L2, R1, R2, Circle, Circle, Square, Square.

TEMPORARY INVULNERABILITY

At the Cheat Menu, press L1 (x6), R2.

FULL ARMOR

At the Cheat Menu, press L1, L1, R1, R1, X, X, Circle, Circle.

UNLIMITED AMMO

At the Cheat Menu, press L2, Circle, R2, Square, Circle, L2, R1.

DOUBLE DAMAGE

At the Cheat Menu, press Square (x3), Circle (x3), X.

INVISIBILITY

At the Cheat Menu, press Square, X, Circle, Square, X, Circle, Square.

LEVEL SELECT ENABLED

At the Cheat Menu, press Circle, X, Square, Square, X, Square, Circle.

ALL WEAPONS

At the Cheat Menu, press R2, X, L1, Square, R1, Circle, L2.

INVULNERABILITY

At the Cheat Menu, press L1, Square, Circle, Circle, Square, L1, L2.

OUTTAKE CINEMATICS

At the Cheat Menu, press L1, L2, R1, R2, Square, Square, Circle, Circle.

ENDING MOVIE

At the Cheat Menu, press Circle, R2, L1, Square, L2, X, R2.

ALL CHEATS

At the Cheat Menu, press L1, L2, R2, R1, L1, L2, R2, R1, L1, L2, R2, R1, L1, L2, R2, R1, Circle (x4), X (x4), Square (x4), Select (x4).

FEAR EFFECT

MAX AMMO

Select Options and then Credits. Then press L1, ▲, Up, Down, ●, ●, ▲, ■, Left, ▲.

INVINCIBLE

Select Options and then Credits. Then press L1, ▲, Up, Down, ●, ●, ▲, ■, Right, ■.

TOUGHER DIFFICULTY

Select Options and then Credits. Then press Down, Down, Down, ▲, Down, Down, Down, ■, Left, Right.

ONE-SHOT KILLS

Select Options and then Credits. Then press L1, ▲, Up, Down, ●, ●, ▲, ■, Down, R1.

PUZZLES COMPLETED

Select Options and then Credits. Then press L1, ▲, Up, Down, ●, ●, Down, Down, Down, Up.

FIGHTING FORCE 2

CHEAT MODE

Press L1 + L2 + R1 + ▲ + X + Left at the Title screen. Start a game and select a level. This gives your character unlimited ammunition and invincibility. **NOTE:** You cannot save your game with this cheat.

Cheat Mode.

GRAND THEFT AUTO 2

For the following codes, enter the cheats as a player name:

CHEAT	EFFECT
BIGSCORE	1,000,000 Points
HIGHFIVE	5X Multiplier
MUCHCASH	500,000 Dollars
LIVELONG	Unlimited Energy
NAVARONE	All Weapons and Ammo

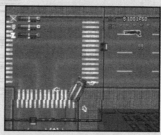

All Weapons and Ammo.

LOSEFEDS	Disable Law Enforcement
DESIRES	Maximum Wanted Level
ITSALLUP	Level Select

Level Select.

CHEAT	EFFECT
WUGGLES	Coordinates Displayed

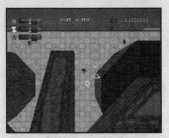

Coordinates Displayed.

NOFRILLS	Debug Mode

HOT WHEELS TURBO RACING

Enter the following codes at the Main Menu. You will hear a sound when entered correctly.

EFFECT	CODE
Infinite Turbos	R2, L1, ■, ▲, R1, L2, L1, R2
Small Cars	■, R2, L2, ▲, ▲, L2, R2, ■

Small Cars.

EFFECT	CODE
Tow Jam Car	■, ▲, L1, R1, L2, R2, ■, ▲

Tow Jam Car.

Large Tires	■, ▲, ■, ▲, R1, R1, L2, L2

Large Tires.

No Textures on Cars	L1, R1, L2, R2, L1, R1, L2, R2

No Textures on Cars.

Weird Sounds	R2, R1, L2, R2, ■, ▲, L1, R1

JARRETT & LABONTE RACING

CHEATS

Enter the following as codes:

CODE	EFFECT
Kerbkrawl	Exploding kerbs
T2	Silver car
Glycerine	Nitro (Press X + Circle to use)
Ethanol	blur
Europa	??
Gruntsome	More Power
Vanishing	??

KNOCKOUT KINGS 2000

FIGHT AS JERMAINE DUPRI

At the Boxer Creation screen, enter **JERMAINE DUPRI** as a name.

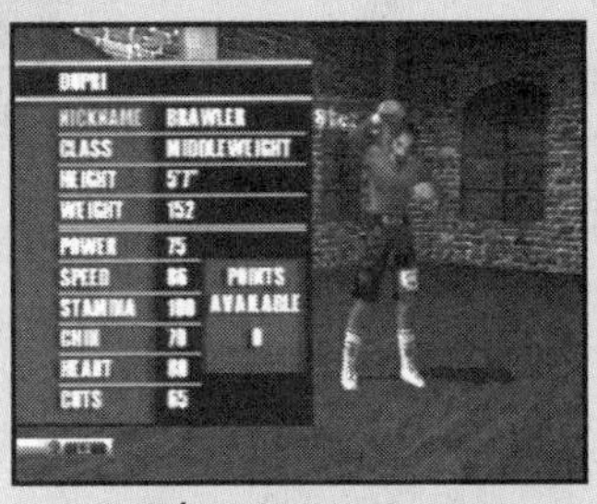

Fight as Jermaine Dupri.

FIGHT AS Q-TIP

At the Boxer Creation screen, enter **Q TIP** as a name.

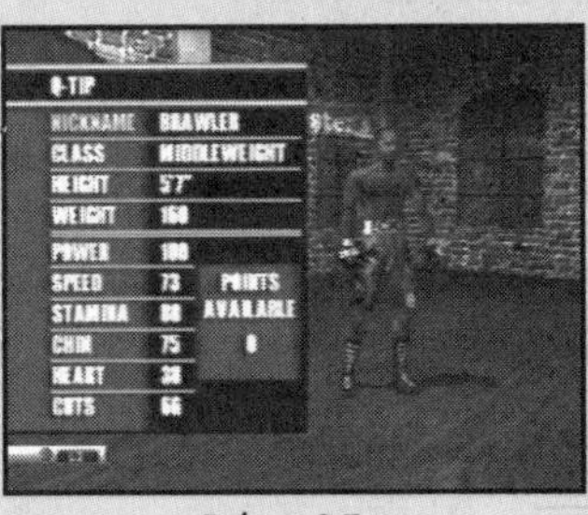

Fight as Q-Tip.

FIGHT AS O

At the Boxer Creation screen, enter **O** as a name.

FIGHT AS MARC ECKO

At the Boxer Creation screen, enter **MARC ECKO** as a name.

FIGHT AS TIM DUNCAN

At the Boxer Creation screen, enter **TIM DUNCAN** as a name.

Fight as Tim Duncan.

FIGHT AS MARLON WAYANS

At the Boxer Creation screen, enter **MARLON WAYANS** as a name.

Fight as Marlon Wayans.

FIGHT AS GARGOYLE

At the Boxer Creation screen, enter **GARGOYLE** as a name.

FIGHT AS ALIEN

At the Boxer Creation screen, enter **ROSWELL** as a name.

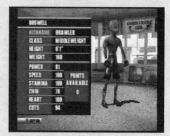

Fight as Alien.

FIGHT AS SHMACKO THE CLOWN

At the Boxer Creation screen, enter **SHMACKO** as a name.

Fight as Shmacko the Clown.

FIGHT AS ED MAHONE

At the Boxer Creation screen, enter **ED MAHONE** as a name.

KURT WARNER'S ARENA FOOTBALL UNLEASHED

To enter the following codes, press the Turbo, Jump, and Pass buttons at the Vs. screen. For example, pressing Turbo enters the first number, Jump enters the second number, and Pass enters the last number. Then press the D-pad in the noted direction.

BIG HEAD

2 0 0 Right

HUGE HEAD

0 4 0 Up

TEAM BIG HEADS

2 0 3 Right

Team Big Heads.

NO HEAD

3 2 1 Left

HEADLESS TEAM

1 2 3 Right

BIG FOOTBALL

0 5 0 Right

PLAYER WITH BALL INVISIBLE

4 3 3 Up

45

TEAM TINY PLAYERS
3 1 0 Right

HIDE RECEIVER NAME
1 0 2 Right

**NO HIGHLIGHTING
(TARGET RECEIVER)**
3 2 1 Down

POWERUP OFFENSE
3 1 2 Up

POWERUP DEFENSE
4 2 1 Up

POWERUP TEAMMATES
4 2 1 Up

**POWERUP SPEED (2-
PLAYER AGREEMENT)**
4 0 4 Left

POWERUP BLOCKERS
3 1 2 Left

HYPER BLITZ
5 5 5 Up

SUPER BLITZING
0 4 5 Up

NO INTERCEPTIONS
3 4 4 Up

NO FIRST DOWNS
2 1 0 Up

FAST PASSES
2 5 0 Left

FAST TURBO RUNNING
0 3 2 Left

INFINITE TURBO
5 1 4 Up

SUPER FIELD GOALS
1 2 3 Left

**TOURNAMENT MODE
(2-PLAYER
AGREEMENT)**
1 1 1 Down

**SUPER PASSING (2-
PLAYER AGREEMENT)**
4 2 3 Right

**SHOW MORE FIELD (2-
PLAYER AGREEMENT)**
0 2 1 Right

NO RANDOM RUMBLES
4 2 3 Down

**DERANGED PLAY (1-
PLAYER GAME)**
2 1 2 Down

**ULTRA HARD (1-
PLAYER GAME)**
3 2 3 Up

**SMART CPU OPPONENT
(1-PLAYER GAME)**
3 1 4 Down

**UNLIMITED THROW
DISTANCES**
2 2 3 Right

LEGO ROCK RAIDERS

PASSWORDS

MISSION	PASSWORD
Bandit's Mission Completed	Down, Triangle, Down, Circle, Up, Down, Square, Triangle, Left, Down, Up, Circle, Triangle, Left, Down, Down, Left, Triangle, Left, Square, Circle, Down
Axle's Mission Completed	Circle, Triangle, Right, Triangle, X, Up, Triangle, Right, Circle, Right, Left. Down, Up, Right, Triangle, Circle, Up, Right, Square, Square, Circle, Right
Jet's Mission Completed	X, Triangle, Right, Triangle, Up, Down, Square, Triangle, Left, Down, Up, Circle, Triangle, Left, Down, Down, Left, Triangle, Left, Up, Circle, Right
Doc's Mission Completed	Up, Square, X, Triangle, Up, Circle, Left, Triangle, Square, Triangle, Left, Down, Circle, Up, Down, Circle, Triangle, Up, Down, Up, Triangle, X
Spark's Mission Completed	Right, Square, Left, Up, X, Down, Circle, Down, Square, Triangle, Up, Down, Circle, Left, Square, Triangle, Triangle, Square, Up, Square, Triangle, Left
Trapped Mission Complete	Triangle, Circle, Right, Triangle, Square, Square, Down, Right, Left, Triangle, Circle, Left, Up, Right, Square, Circle, Triangle, Circle, Triangle, Triangle, Triangle, Right

A B C D E F G H I J K L M N O P Q R S T U V W X Y Z

MADDEN NFL 2000

Enter the following codes at the Code Entry screen:

EFFECT	CODE
More Injuries	PAINFUL
Large vs. Small	MINIME
20 Yards to 1st Down	FIRSTIS20
No Interceptions	EXPRESSBALL
Blind Referee	REFISBLIND
The QB Is in the Club	QBINTHECLUB
Dodge City: Old West Stadium	WILDWEST

Old West Stadium.

EA Sports Stadium	ITSINTHEGAME

EA Sports Stadium.

EFFECT	CODE
Fantasy Team: Marshalls	COWBOYS

Fantasy Team: Marshalls.

All 60s Team	MOJOBABY
All 70s Team	LOVEBEADS
Great Game 1: 81 Dolphins	15MOREMIN
Great Game 1: 81 Chargers	BUILDMONKEYS
Great Game 2: 76 Raiders	GAMMALIGHT
Great Game 2: 76 Patriots	HACKCHEESE
Great Game 3: 97 Packers	TUNDRA
Great Game 3: 97 Broncos	EARTHPEOPLE
Great Game 4: 85 Dolphins	CHICKIN
Great Game 4: 85 Bears	DOORKNOB
Great Game 5: 90 Giants	PROFSMOOTH
Great Game 5: 90 Bills	SPOON
Great Game 6: 86 Browns	KAMEHAMEHA
Great Game 6: 86 Broncos	BLUESCREEN
Great Game 7: 88 49ers	CALLMESALLY
Great Game 7: 88 Bengals	PTMOMINFOGET
Great Game 8: 72 Steelers	DONTGOFOR2
Great Game 8: 72 Raiders	GETMEADOCTOR
Great Game 9: 95 Steelers	STEAMPUNK
Great Game 9: 95 Colts	PREDATORS

B
C
D
E
F
G
H
I
J
K
L
M
N
O
P
Q
R
S
T
U
V
W
X
Y
Z

MEDAL OF HONOR: UNDERGROUND

MOHU TEAM PICTURES

Enter **MOHUEQUIPE** as a password at the Options menu.

Mohu Team
X-Mas '99.

CARTOON GALLERY

Enter **MOHDESSINS** as a password at the Options menu.

DREAMWORKS INTERACTIVE PICTURES

Enter **DWIECRANS** as a password at the Options menu.

MEDIEVIL II

CHEAT MENU

Pause the game, hold L2 and press ▲, ●, ▲, ●, ●, ▲, Left, ●, Up, Down, Right, ●, Left, Left, ▲, Right, ●, Left, Left, ▲, ●, Down, ●, ●, Right. The cheat option will appear on the pause menu.

Cheat Menu.

MTV SPORTS: SKATEBOARDING

UNLOCK CHARACTERS, BOARDS AND LEVELS

Enter the name **PASWRD**.

MUPPET: RACE MANIA

ALL CHARACTERS AND VEHICLES

At the title screen press Triangle, Circle, Triangle, Square, Triangle, X, Triangle, Triangle, X, Circle.

ALL COURSES

At the title screen press Circle, Triangle, X, Circle, Triangle, X, Circle, Triangle, Square, X.

ARCHES COURSE

At the title screen press Square, Circle, X, Circle, Sqaure, Triangle, Circle, X, Circle, Triangle. This also puts food on every course.

STUDIO COURSE

At the title screen press Square, Square, Circle, Circle, X, Circle, Triangle, Circle, Triangle, Square. This also puts stars on every course.

ALL DOZERS AND FRAGGLE ROCK BONUS COURSE

At the title screen press X, Square, X, Square, X, Square, Triangle, Circle, X, Square.

END CREDITS AND EXTRA COURSES

At the title screen press Circle, Triangle, Square, Triangle, X, Triangle, Square, Circle Triangle, X.

RESET

At the title screen press Triangle, X, Circle, X, Square, Square, X, Circle, X, Triangle. Be careful this resets the game.

NASCAR 2000

NASCAR LEGENDS

To access one of the following drivers, highlight Select Car and enter the following:

DRIVER	CODE
Bobby Allison	L1, R1, L1, R1, ■, L2, R2, L2, R2, ●

Bobby Allison.

Davey Allison	R1, L1, R1, L1, ■, R2, L2, R2, L2, ●
Alan Kulwicki	L1, R1, L2, R2, ■, R1, L1, R2, L2, ●
Benny Parsons	L1, R2, R1, L2, ■, R2, L1, R1, L2, ●

Benny Parsons.

DRIVER	CODE
David Pearson	L1, R1, R2, L2, ■, R1, L1, L2, R2, ●
Cale Yarborough	L1, L2, R1, R2, ■, R1, R2, L1, L2, ●

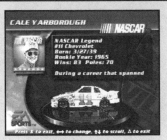

Cale Yarborough.

BIG SKY RACEWAY MONTANA

Highlight Select Car, and press L1, L1, R1, R1, ■, L2, L2, R2, R2, ●.

NASCAR RUMBLE

ALL CARS AND COURSES

Enter **C9P5AU8NAA** as a password at the Load and Save Game Option.

All Cars and Courses

NBA LIVE 2000

LEGENDARY PLAYERS

At the Game Setup screen, press ●, highlight the player icon, press Right, and then press X to select Create Player. Enter the following first and last names and press X to accept the entry. You will see a message when entered correctly. Then at the Game Setup screen, press ●, highlight the star icon, and press X. You can add a legend to the Free Agent list by pressing X while on that player.

PLAYER	ERA	FIRST NAME	LAST NAME
Andrew Phillip	50s	Whiz	Kid
Bill Sharman	50s	Charity	Stripe
Bob Cousy	50s	B-Balls	Cooz
Bob Pettit	50s	Crash	Boards
Carl Braun	50s	Hard	Wood
Cliff Hagen	50s	Hook	Shot
Dolph Schayes	50s	Set	Shot
George Yardley	50s	Yard	Bird
Harry Gallatin	50s	Iron	Horse
Larry Costello	50s	Cross	Over
Paul Arizin	50s	Pitchin'	Philli
Richard Guerin	50s	Play	Maker
Bill Russell	60s	All	Defensive
Elgin Baylor	60s	Offensive	Force
Hal Greer	60s	Jump	Shot
Jerry Lucas	60s	Lucas	Layup
Jerry West	60s	The Mr.	Clutch
Lenny Wilkins	60s	Player	Coach
Oscar Robertson	60s	Bucks	Big O
Sam Jones	60s	Bank	Shot
Tommy Heinsohn	60s	Flat	Shot
Walt Bellamy	60s	No	Comment
Willis Reed	60s	Soft	Touch
Wilt Chamberlain	60s	Big	Goliath
Bill Walton	70s	Shot	Blocker
Billy Cunningham	70s	Leaping	Kangaroo
Bob Lanier	70s	Big	Foot
Dave Bing	70s	The	Duke
Dave Cowens	70s	Red	Head
Earl Monroe	70s	Magic	Pearl
John Havlicek	70s	John	Hondo
Nate Archibald	70s	Big	Tiny
Pete Maravich	70s	Passing	Pistol
Rick Barry	70s	Foul	Shot
Walt Frazier	70s	Cool	Clyde
Wes Unseld	70s	Glass	Cleaner

PLAYER	ERA	FIRST NAME	LAST NAME
Charles Barkley	80s	Mound of	Rebound
Dominique Wilkins	80s	High	Light
Earvin Johnson	80s	Magical	Guard
George Gervin	80s	Chilled	Iceman
Hakeem Olajuwon	80s	The Dream	Machine
Isiah Thomas	80s	Bad Boy	Zeke
James Worthy	80s	Big	Game
Julius Erving	80s	Doctor's	In
Kevin McHale	80s	Sixth	Man
Larry Bird	80s	Celtics	Pride
Michael Jordan	80s	Come Fly	With Me
Moses Malone	80s	Free	Throws
Robert Parish	80s	Celtic	Chief
David Robinson	90s	Spurs	Admiral
Gary Payton	90s	Human	Glove
Grant Hill	90s	Class	Act
John Stockton	90s	Jazz	Man
Karl Malone	90s	Mailman	Delivers
Mitch Richmond	90s	Live	Coverman
Patrick Ewing	90s	Player	President
Reggie Miller	90s	Outside	Threat
Scottie Pippen	90s	Complete	Game
Shaquille O'Neal	90s	Little	Warrior
Shawn Kemp	90s	Power	Dunker

NBA SHOWTIME

CHANGE COURT

To select a court, choose a player, and then press the following at the Player Select screen.

COURT	PRESS
Home Team Court	Turbo + Up
Away Team Court	Turbo + Down

A B C D E F G H I J K L M N O P Q R S T U V W X Y Z

COURT	PRESS
Street Court	Turbo + Left
Island Court	Turbo + Right

Island Court.

Midway Court	Shoot + Pass + Up

CHEAT CODES

To enter the following codes, you must press the Turbo, Shoot, and Pass buttons at the Today's Match-Up screen. Pressing Turbo enters the first number, Shoot enters the second number, and Pass enters the last number. Then press the D-pad in the noted direction. For example, to enter the **No Hotspots** code you would press Turbo (X2), Pass (X1), and then press Up.

EFFECT	CODE
No Hotspots	2 0 1 Up
Show Hotspots	1 0 0 Down

Show Hotspots.

No Player Arrow	3 2 1 Left
Tournament Mode	1 1 1 Down
Show Shot Percentage	0 0 1 Down

EFFECT	CODE
No Goaltending	5 5 5 Left
Big Head Mode	2 0 0 Right

Big Head Mode.

Tiny Heads	4 4 0 Left
Tiny Players	3 4 5 Left
ABA Ball	2 3 2 Right
Infinite Turbo	4 1 1 Up
No Fouls	2 2 2 Right
Midway Uniform	4 0 1 Right
Team Uniform	4 0 0 Right
Home Uniform	4 1 0 Right
Away Uniform	4 2 0 Right
Alternate Uniform	4 3 0 Right

HIDDEN PLAYERS

To access the following hidden players, enter their name and pin number:

CHARACTER	NAME	PIN #
Kerri Hoskins	KERRI	0220
Kerri (Alternate Uniform)	KERRI	1111
Lia Montelongo	LIA	0712
Lia (Alternate Uniform)	LIA	1111
Retro Rob	RETRO	1970
Pinto Horse	PINTO	1966
White Horse	HORSE	1966
Small Alien	SMALLS	0856
Large Alien	BIGGY	0958
Nikko the Devil Dog	NIKKO	6666

B C D E F G H I J K L M N O P Q R S T U V W X Y Z

CHARACTER	NAME	PIN #
Old Man	OLDMAN	2001
Crispy the Clown	CRISPY	2084
Pumpkin	JACKO	1031
Wizard	THEWIZ	1136
Referee	THEREF	7777

NBA MASCOTS

MASCOT	NAME	PIN
Atlanta Hawks	HAWK	0322
Chicago Bulls	BENNY	0503
Charlotte Hornets	HORNET	1105
Denver Nuggets	ROCKY	0201
Houston Rockets	TURBO	1111
Indiana Pacers	BOOMER	0604
Minnesota Timberwolves	CRUNCH	0503
New Jersey Nets	SLY	6765
Phoenix Suns	GORILA	0314
Seattle Supersonics	SASQUA	7785
Toronto Raptors	RAPTOR	1020
Utah Jazz	BEAR	1228

THE MIDWAY GANG

CHARACTER	CODE	PIN
Mark Turmell	TURMEL	0322
Rob Gatson	GATSON	1111
Mark Guidarelli	GUIDO	6765
Dan Thompson	DANIEL	0604
Jeff Johnson	JAPPLE	6660
Jason Skiles	JASON	3141
Sal DiVita	SAL	0201
Jennifer Hedrick	JENIFR	3333
Jennifer Hedrick (Alternate Uniform)	JENIFR	1111
Eugene Geer	E GEER	1105
Matt Gilmore	MATT G	1006

CHARACTER	CODE	PIN
Tim Bryant	TIMMYB	3314
Jim Gentile	GENTIL	1228
John Root	ROOT	6000
Jon Hey	JONHEY	8823
Andy Eloff	ELOFF	2181
Mike Lynch	LYNCH	3333
Paulo Garcia	PAULO	0517
Brian LeBaron	GRINCH	0222
Alex Gilliam	LEX	0014
Jim Tianis	DIMI	0619
Dave Grossman	DAVE	1104
Larry Wotman	STRAT	2112
Chris Skrundz	CMSVID	0000
Beth Smukowski	BETHAN	1111
Paul Martin	STENTR	0269
Shawn Liptak	LIPTAK	0114
Isiah Thomas	THOMAS	1111
Tim Kitzrow	TIMK	7785
Willie Morris	WIL	0101
Greg Cutler	CUTLER	1111
Chad Edmunds	CHAD	0628
Tim Moran	TIMCRP	6666

NCAA FOOTBALL 2000

For the following codes, choose the Secret Codes option in the Game Options and enter the following:

Secret Codes.

EFFECT	CODE
Super Stats Team	UNSTOPPABLE
Faster Daylight Effects	TIMEFLIES
Maximum Recruiting Points	STAFFUP
All Exhibition Mode Stadiums	STADSGALORE
Defense Always Intercepts	PIXGALORE
Extra Long Kicks	ICBM
Faster Gameplay	SCRAMBLE
Receivers Always Catch Ball	GIMMEDABALL
View CPU Plays	MINDREADER
Maximum Wind	SAFETY
Defense Always Tackles	BRICKWALL
Maximum Attribute Points	BLUECHIP

Maximum Attribute Points.

View Intro Sequence	BIGSCREEN
View Entire Rankings	CONTROVERSY
Knock Down Referee for 1 Point	BADCALL

Knock Down Ref.

EFFECT	CODE
Change Title to NCAA 1900	Y2K
1946 Notre Dame	GOLDPAINT
1947 Army	INSIDEOUTSIDE
1957 Notre Dame	STREAKOVER
1957 Oklahoma	FORTYSEVENNONE
1959 LSU	RIGHTTHISTIME
1959 Mississippi	HEYREB
1962 USC	FIGHTFORTROY
1962 Wisconsin	BUCKY
1965 Michigan State	BIGGREEN
1965 UCLA	REVENGE
1966 Michigan State	NEEDAWIN
1966 Notre Dame	TAKETHETIE
1967 USC	WHITEHORSE
1967 UCLA	PRESSBOX
1968 Ohio State	5TITLES
1968 USC	NICERUN
1969 Arkansas	WOOPIGSOOEY
1969 Texas	TEXASFIGHT
1970 Ohio State	BRUTUS
1970 Stanford	MVPQB
1971 Nebraska	GAMEOFCENTURY
1971 Oklahoma	SCHOONER
1973 Alabama	PLAYTHEPASS
1973 Michigan	RUNNERUP
1973 Notre Dame	GUTSYCALL
1973 Ohio State	WINNINGVOTE
1974 Notre Dame	LOSTLEAD
1974 USC	RALLY
1975 Arizona State	DEJAVU
1975 Nebraska	HERBIE
1976 Georgia	HEDGES
1976 Pittsburgh	RUSHTD
1978 Alabama	GOALLINESTAND
1978 Penn State	SHOULDAPASSED

A B C D E F G H I J K L M N O P Q R S T U V W X Y Z

EFFECT	CODE
1979 Ohio State	JUSTSHORT
1979 USC	MVPRUN
1981 Clemson	TOUCHTHEROCK
1981 North Carolina	NOTHINGFINER
1982 Cal	THEPLAY
1982 Georgia	SICEMDAWGS
1982 Penn State	LIONPRIDE
1982 Stanford	TROMBONE
1983 Miami	KNOCKITDOWN
1983 Nebraska	GOFOR2
1984 Boston College	MIRACLE
1984 Miami	BADLUCK
1985 Alabama	BLOCKTHATKICK
1985 Auburn	SMARTBACK
1985 Oklahoma	UPSETLIONS
1985 Penn State	SOONERLATER
1986 Penn State	LINEBACKERINT
1986 Miami	FATIGUES
1987 Miami	MONSTERD
1987 Oklahoma	SLOWSTART
1988 Notre Dame	LEPRECHAUN
1988 UCLA	LBBRUINS
1988 USC	TROJANWAR
1988 West Virginia	HURTQB
1989 Alabama	TOOMUCHD
1989 Colorado	MISSEDCHANCES
1989 Notre Dame	LIFTOFF
1991 Miami	SHUTOUT
1991 Michigan	NICEPOSE
1991 Nebraska	HITTHEWEIGHTS
1991 Washington	WILDDOGS
1992 Alabama	REALMENPLAYZONE
1992 Miami	TOOTALENTED
1993 Florida State	TOMAHAWK
1993 Nebraska	REFUSELOSE
1994 Miami	RUNOUTSIDE

EFFECT	CODE
1994 Nebraska	STEAMROLLER
1994 Oregon	GREENGANG
1994 Penn State	ALMOSTNO.1
1996 Florida	PUTINLARRY
1996 Florida State	GETTHEQB
1997 Washington State	TURNOVER
1997 Nebraska	CORNFED
1997 Michigan	SPLITVOTE
1997 Tennessee	SMOKEY
All Tiburon Team	LASERBEAMS
All EA Sports Team	INTHEGAME

NCAA GAMEBREAKER 2001

EASTER EGGS

Select Customize and then Easter Eggs to enter the following case-sensitive codes:

EFFECT	CODE
Version	Vers
One team bigger than other	BIGandsmall

Attributes at 99	BEAT DOWN
Better Passing	GO DEEP
Better Running	REAL ESTATE
Strong Stiff Arm	HAMMER

EFFECT	CODE
Stronger Defense	PHYSICAL
Better Walk-on Players	FRANKENSTEIN
All Blue Chips	motivate
Credits	HOLLYWOOD

NFL BLITZ 2001

VS CHEATS

You must enter the following codes at the Versus screen by pressing the Turbo, Jump, and Pass buttons. For example, to get Infinite Turbo press Turbo (x5), Jump (x1), Pass (x4), and then press Up.

EFFECT	CODE
Tournament Mode (2-player game)	1,1,1 Down
Infinite Turbo	5,1,4 Up
Fast Turbo Running	0,3,2 Left
Power-up Offense	3,1,2 Up
Power-up Defense	4,2,1 Up
Power-up Teammates	2,3,3 Up
Power-up Blockers	3,1,2 Left
Super Blitzing	0,4,5 Up
Super Field Goals	1,2,3 Left
Invisible	4,3,3 Up

No Random Fumbles	4,2,3 Down
No First Downs	2,1,0 Up
No Interceptions	3,4,4 Up
No Punting	1,5,1 Up

EFFECT	CODE
Allow Stepping Out of Bounds	2,1,1 Left
Fast Passes	2,5,0 Left
Late Hits	0,1,0 Up
Show Field Goal %	0,0,1 Down
Show Punt Hangtime Meter	0,0,1 Right
Hide Receiver Name	1,0,2 Right
Big Football	0,5,0 Right
Big Head	2,0,0 Right
Huge Head	0,4,0 Up

Team Tiny Players	3,1,0 Right
Team Big Players	1,4,1 Right
Team Big Heads	2,0,3 Right

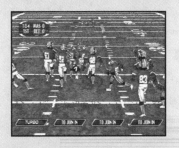

Weather: Snow	5,2,5 Down
Weather: Rain	5,5,5 Right
No Hiliting on Target Receiver	3,2,1 Down
Red, White and Blue Ball	3,2,3 Left
Unlimited Throw Distance	2,2,3 Right
Deranged Blitz Mode (1-player game)	2,1,2 Down

EFFECT	CODE
Ultra Hard Mode (1-player game)	3,2,3 Up
Smart CPU Opponent (1-player game)	3,1,4 Down
Always Quarterback	2,2,2 Left
Always Receiver	2,2,2 Right
Cancel Always Quarterback/Receiver	3,3,3 Up
Show More Field (2-player agreement)	0,2,1 Right
No CPU Assistance (2-player agreement)	0,1,2 Down
Power-up Speed (2-player agreement)	4,0,4 Left
Hyper Blitz (2-player agreement)	5,5,5 Up
No Play Selection (2-player agreement)	1,1,5 Left
Super Passing (2-player agreement)	4,2,3 Right

TEAM PLAYBOOKS

Arizona Cardinals	1,0,1 Left
Atlanta Falcons	1,0,2 Left
Baltimore Ravens	1,0,3 Left
Buffalo Bills	1,0,4 Left
Carolina Panthers	1,0,5 Left
Chicago Bears	1,1,0 Left
Cincinnati Bengals	1,1,2 Left
Cleveland Browns	1,1,3 Left
Dallas Cowboys	1,1,4 Left
Denver Broncos	1,1,5 Right
Detroit Lions	1,2,1 Left
Green Bay Packers	1,2,2 Left
Indianapolis Colts	1,2,3 Up
Jacksonville Jaguars	1,2,4 Left
Kansas City Chiefs	1,2,5 Left
Miami Dolphins	1,3,1 Left
Minnesota Vikings	1,3,2 Left
New England Patriots	1,3,3 Left
New Orleans Saints	1,3,4 Left
New York Giants	1,3,5 Left
New York Jets	1,4,1 Left
Oakland Raiders	1,4,2 Left

EFFECT	CODE
Philadelphia Eagles	1,4,3 Left
Pittsburgh Steelers	1,4,4 Left
San Diego Chargers	1,4,5 Left
San Francisco 49ers	1,5,1 Left
Seattle Seahawks	1,5,2 Left
St. Louis Rams	1,5,3 Left
Tampa Bay Buccaneers	1,5,4 Left
Tennessee Titans	1,5,5 Left
Washington Redskins	2,0,1 Left

NFL GAMEDAY 2001

CHEAT MODE

Enter the following at the Easter Egg menu. Note that _ is a space:

EFFECT	CODE
Bad CPU	CHEATERS
Expert Mode	SMARTER_CPU
Unbeatable Team	UNBEATABLE
Opponent Kicks Only 20 Yards	AIR_CPU
More Hits	JACK_HAMMER
More Injuries	HAM_INJURY
Speed Bursts for Ball Carrier	ROCKET_MAN
Even Players	ALL_EVEN
More Endurance	ENDURANCE
Receivers with Great Hands	STICKEM
Harder and Longer Passes	SHOOTERS
Harder Tackles	CRUNCH
Improved Defensive Line	LINE_BUSTER
Improved Running Back	SUPER_FOOT
Faster Players	BOOSTER
Quicker Fatigue	FATIGUE
Flat Players	TWO_D
Small Players	FLEA_CIRCUS

A
B
C
D
E
F
G
H
I
J
K
L
M
N
O
P
Q
R
S
T
U
V
W
X
Y
Z

EFFECT	CODE
Small, Fast Players	POP_WARNER
Tall, Skinny Players	STICK_MEN

Huge Players	GIANTS
Big Football	BIG_PIG
Credits	CREDITS

GameDay Field	GD_FIELD
989 Studios Players	989_SPORTS
Bobo Players	ALL_BOBO

EFFECT	CODE
Basketball Players	BASKETBALL
European League Stars	EURO_LEAGUE
Programmers	RED_ZONE
U.S. Presidents Names	OVAL_OFFICE

Last Season's Players	OLD_SCHOOL
Frame-by-Frame Movement	STROBE_LIGHT
Cheerleaders After Game	FASHION_SHOW

SUPER BOWL TEAMS AND ALL-STAR TEAMS

At the Team Select screen, press Circle All-Star teams. Press Circle (x2) for Super Bowl teams.

NO FEAR DOWNHILL MOUNTAIN BIKE RACING

CHEAT CODES

Select Time Trial, choose "Yes" for the access code, and enter the following:

CODE	ENTER
Mirror Mode	EDOMRORRIM
Trick Trail	MONKEYBIKE
Alien Trail	ABDUCTION
All Trails	LOTSOFFEAR
Cartoon Trail	TOONITUP
Virtual Reality Trail	JACKEDIN
All Upgrades	LOTSOFGEAR
All Riders	GOOBERS
Moon Gravity	BIGFLOATER
Wire Frame	TIREFRAME

POWER RANGERS: LIGHTSPEED RESCUE

TITANIUM RANGER

Enter **ULTIMATE 800B39940001** as a code.

LEVEL SKIP

Enter **OMEGA** as a code.

PRO PINBALL BIG RACE USA

PASSENGER FRENZY WITH 15 BALLS

Select Side Show and then press Circle, Square, Left (x6), Start.

QUAKE II

INVINCIBILITY

Pause the game and press L2, L2, R1, R2, R1, L2.

RAINBOW SIX

REVIVE ALL OPERATIVES

At the Main Menu, press and hold L1, and press ▲, ▲, X, ●, ●, X, ■, ■.

TOGGLE INVINCIBLE HOSTAGES

Pause the game, press and hold L1, and press ●, ●, ■, ▲, X, ▲, X, ●. You can also enter this code at the Main Menu.

RESTORE AMMO

Pause the game, press and hold L1, and press ■, ■, ●, ▲, X, ▲, X, ▲.

SECONDARY WEAPONS

Pause the game, press and hold L1, and press X, ▲, ■, ●, ■, X, ▲, ■. You can enter the code again for the next secondary weapon. These include the Beretta, HK .40, HK .45 and the silenced versions.

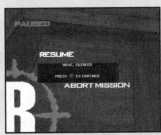

Secondary Field.

TOGGLE NO LOCKED DOORS

Pause the game, press and hold L1 and press ▲, ■, ■, ▲ X, ●, ■, ▲. You can also enter this code at the Main Menu.

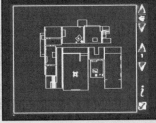

Toggle Reveal Map.

TOGGLE REVEAL MAP

Pause the game, press and hold L1, and press X, ●, ■, ▲, ▲, ■, ●, X. You can also enter this code at the Main Menu.

ALL ATTRIBUTES SET TO MAXIMUM

Pause the game, press and hold L1, and press X, ■, ▲, ▲, ●, ■, X, X. You can also enter this code at the Main Menu.

TOGGLE VICTORY CONDITIONS

Pause the game, press and hold L1, and press ●, ▲, ▲, X, ●, ■, X, ▲. You can also enter this code at the Main Menu.

CREDITS PREVIEW

At the Main Menu, press and hold L1, and press ■, ▲, ■, ■, ●, ●, X, ▲.

TOGGLE NO TERRORISTS

Pause the game, press and hold L1, and press ▲, ●, ●, ▲, ■,

Credits Preview.

X, ▲, ●. You can also enter this code at the Main Menu.

RAMPAGE THROUGH TIME

ACCESS MOVIES IN CHEAT MENU

Enter the password 12345. Select Cheats in the Options to find the movies.

FULL POWER METER

Enter the password JOSHS.

RC STUNT COPTER

UNLOCK LEVELS

At the Main Menu press Down, Up, Right, Left, ▲, X, ■, ●. You will hear "Cheaters Never Prosper" when entered correctly.

ALL GOLD

At the Main Menu press Down, Up, Left, Right, ▲, X, ■, ●. You will hear "Cheaters Never Prosper" when entered correctly.

All Gold.

MEGA POINTS

At the Main Menu press L2, R2, L1, R1, ▲, ●, X, ■. You will hear "Cheaters Never Prosper" when entered correctly.

LONGER NAME

At the Main Menu press Up, Down, Left, Right, ▲, X, ■, ●. You will hear "Cheaters Never Prosper" when entered correctly.

Longer Name.

ROLLCAGE STAGE 2

ALL TRACKS, CARS, MODES, AND MORE

Enter **I.WANT.IT.ALL.AND.I.WANT.IT.NOW!** as your password.

ATD GHOST CARS

Enter **WLL.IF.IT.AINT.THEM.PESKY.KIDS** as your password.

DEMOLITION MODES

Enter **IS.IT.COLD.IN.HERE.OR.IS.IT.JUST.ME?** as your password.

MEGA SPEED

Enter **LOOK.OUT!.ITS.ANDY.GREEN** as your password.

MIRROR MODE

Enter **I.AM.THE.MIRROR.MAN,.OOOOOOOOOO!** as your password.

PURSUIT MODE

Enter **PURSUIT,.A.SUIT.MADE.FROM.CATS** as your password.

RUBBLE SOCCER MODE

Enter **IM.OBVIOUSLY.SICK.AS.A.PARROT** as your password.

SURVIVOR MODE

Enter **HERE.TODAY,.GONE,.LATE.AFTERNOON** as your password.

ALL COMBAT TRACKS

Enter **YOU.HAVE.A.LOTA.EXPLODING.TO.DO** as your password.

ALL TRACKS

Enter **NOW.THAT'S.WHAT.I.CALL.RACING.147** as your password.

ALL CARS

Enter **WHEELS,.METAL,.ITS.....THE.BIN!** as your password.

MORE DIFFICULT MASTERS

Enter **MASTERS.IS.AS.HARD.AS.NAILS.MON!** as your password.

SLED STORM

To enter the following codes, you must access the Password screen from the Memory Card menu in the options.

PLAY AS JACKAL

At the Password screen, press L2, L2, ●, R2, ■, R1, L1, ▲.

PLAY AS SERGEI

At the Password screen, press ■, L1, ■, L2, ▲, R2, X, ●.

RYAN'S STORM SLED

At the Password screen, press ●, ▲, ■, R2, R2, L1, X, ▲.

GIO'S SLED STORM

At the Password screen, press ●, ▲, ■, L1, R2, L1, X, ▲.

JAY'S SLED STORM

At the Password screen, press ●, ▲, ■, ●, R2, L1, X, ▲.

NADIA'S SLED STORM

At the Password screen, press ●, ▲, ■, ■, R2, L1, X, ▲.

TRACEY'S SLED STORM

At the Password screen, press ●, ▲, ■, ▲, R2, L1, X, ▲.

TRAVIS' SLED STORM

At the Password screen, press ●, ▲, ■, R1, R2, L1, X, ▲.

JACKAL'S SLED STORM

At the Password screen, press ●, ▲, ■, L2, R2, L1, X, ▲. To access this code, you must first Unlock Jackal.

SERGEI'S SLED STORM

At the Password screen, press ●, ▲, ■, X, R2, L1, X, ▲. To access this code, you must first unlock Sergei.

Ryan's Storm Sled.

Nadia's Sled Storm.

Jackal's Slead Storm.

CHEAPER SLED UPGRADES

At the Password screen, press **X**, **L1**, **●**, **▲**, **■**, **■**, **▲**, **L2**.

Cheaper Sled Upgrades.

MIRRORED TRACKS

At the Password screen, press **●**, **L1**, **R2**, **R2**, **R1**, **X**, **▲**, **L2**. You can toggle this option on and off at the Track Select screen.

REVERSED TRACKS

At the Password screen, press **■**, **L1**, **X**, **■**, **R2**, **X**, **▲**, **●**.

SUPER SNOCROSS 4-6

At the Password screen, press **R2**, **▲**, **X**, **R2**, **▲**, **■**, **●**, **X**.

DEMO TRACK

At the Password screen, press **R2**, **L1**, **▲**, **■**, **▲**, **R1**, **●**, **X**.

OPEN MOUNTAIN CHAMPIONSHIP COMPLETE

At the Password screen, press **■**, **X**, **R2**, **■**, **●**, **R1**, **●**, **▲**.

SPACE INVADERS

FIVE SHOTS

Pause the game and press Down, Left, **●**, Down, Right, Right, Right.

NINE LIVES

Pause the game and press Right, Right, Right, Down, **●**, Left, Down.

SPIDER-MAN

BIG HEAD

Select Special/Cheats and enter **DULUX**.

INVINCIBLE

Select Special/Cheats and enter **RUSTCRST**.

LEVEL SELECT

Select Special/Cheats and enter **XCLSIOR**. This also opens up a new option in the Cheats menu.

UNLIMITED WEBBING

Select Special/Cheats and enter **STRUDL**.

UNLOCK COMIC BOOK COVERS IN GALLERY

Select Special/Cheats and enter **ALLSIXCC**.

UNLOCK MOVIES IN GALLERY

Select Special/Cheats and enter **WATCH EM**.

UNLOCK J JAMES JEWETT IN GALLERY

Select Special/Cheats and enter **RULUR**.

UNLOCK EVERYTHING

Select Special/Cheats and enter **EEL NATS**.

STAR TREK: INVASION

VIEW CREDITS

During a mission briefing, press Left, Right, Up, Down (x5).

STAR WARS DEMOLITION

Select Options from the Main menu, choose Preferences and press and hold L1 and R1.

PASSCODE	DESCRIPTION
RAISE_THEM	Invincibility
WATTO_SHOP	All vehicles
FIRERATEUP	No delay on weapon fire
NO_PEEKING	Randomly selected opponents and stage

B C D E F G H I J K L M N O P Q R S T U V W X Y Z

STAR WARS EPISODE 1: THE PHANTOM MENACE

TEST DROID CHEAT MENU

At the Main Menu, highlight Options and press ▲, ●, Left, L1, R2, ■, ●, Left. You will hear a sound when entered correctly. Hold L1 + Select + ▲ to access the menu.

STREET SK8ER 2

ALL BOARDS

At the Main Menu, press ●, ●, ■, ●, ■, ■, ●, R1.

All Boards.

ALL COURSES

At the Main Menu, press Left, Right, Left, Right, ●, ●, R1, ■.

ALL CHARACTERS

At the Main Menu, press Left, Left, ●, ●, L2, ■, Right, R2.

MOVIES

At the Main Menu, press R2, R2, L1, L2, L1, R1, R1, R1.

All Characters.

TRICK LEVEL MAX & FULL SKILL POINTS

At the Main Menu, press L1, ■, Left, Left, R2, Left, R1, Left.

SUPERCROSS 2000

At the Main Menu, press R1 and enter the following codes:

CODE	ENTER
Big Bikes	B1GB1K3S

Big Bikes.

Never Crash	NOCR4SH
Bikes Only	NOR1D3RS
Extra Camera Modes	MOR3C4MS
Riders Get in Your Way	BLOCKM3
Bigger Dirt Spray	B1GSPR4Y

Bigger Dirt Spray.

EFFECT	CODE
No More Off-Track	NOOFFTR4CK
No More Resets	SK1PP1NGOK
Giants on Mini-Bikes	G14NTS

Giants on Mini-Bikes.

No Heads	H34DL3SS
Add Hop Button	HOP
Supercross on Mercury	M3RCVRY
Supercross on Venus	V3NVS
Supercross on the Moon	MOON
Supercross on Mars	M4RS
Supercross on Jupiter	JVP1T3R
Supercross on Saturn	S4TVRN
Supercross on Uranus	VR4NVS
Supercross on Neptune	N3PTVN3
Supercross on Pluto	PLVTO

SUPERCROSS CIRCUIT

For the following codes, select Arcade Mode/Bonus Items:

EFFECT	CODE
Headless Rider	SLEEPYHOLLOW

Headless Rider.

Big Helmets	BIG_HELMETS
Invisible Bikes	FLOATING

Invisible Bikes.

SYPHON FILTER 2

END LEVEL

Pause the game, highlight Map and press Right + L2 + R2 + ● + ■ + X. Select Options and then Cheats to find the End Level cheat.

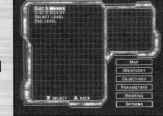

End Level.

VIEW MOVIES

Pause the game, highlight Briefing and press Right + L1 + R2 + ● + X. Select Options and then Cheats to find the Disc 1 and Disc 2 Movies cheats. This will not unlock the movies opened by defeating the hard difficulty.

View Movies.

TARZAN

CHEAT OPTION

At the Main menu, press Left, Left, Right, Right, Up, Down, Left, Right, Up, Up, Down, Down. Then press Down to move below the "Load Game" option to access the "Cheat" option. Press X to select that option for various cheats. Note that you must press Right when selecting a level to display extra levels.

Cheat Option.

LEVEL SELECT

To access this code, you must enable the Cheat Option code. Press L1, R1, L1, R1, L1, R1, L1, R1, L2, R2 at the Cheat Menu. You will hear a sound when entered correctly.

Level Select.

UNLIMITED LIVES

To access this code, you must enable the Cheat Option code. Press L1, R1, L2, R2, L1, R1, L2, R2 at the Cheat Menu.

TENCHU II: BIRTH OF THE STEALTH ASSASSINS

UNLOCK TATSUMARU

At the Mission Select screen, hold Circle and Square and then press R1, R2, L2, L1, Up, Down, Left, Right, Select. This also unlocks Tatsumaru for the Mission Editor.

UNLOCK ALL STAGES

At the Mission Select screen, hold Circle, Square, and Select and then press Right (x3), Up, Left, Down, R2. If Tatsumaru hasn't been unlocked, this will only unlock Ayame's and Rikimaru's missions.

UNLOCK ALL ITEMS

At the Item Select screen, press Square (x3), Circle, Square, Circle, Circle, Left, Up, Down, Right, R2, R2.

INCREASE ITEM INVENTORY BY ONE

At the Item Select screen, hold R1 and Square and then press Right, Down, Left, Up. This adds 1 item to the inventory of all items you currently possess.

RESTORE HEALTH TO 100

During gameplay, pause the game and hold Square and then press Left, Right, Up, Down. Each use of this cheat counts as one "Spotted" in the final score.

SHOW ENTIRE MAP

During gameplay, hold Select and then press Circle (x5). This enables you to briefly view the entire map.

UNLOCK ALL MISSIONS IN MISSION EDITOR

At the Custom Missions Select screen, hold R2 and Circle and then press Up, Down, Down, Right, Left, Left. This doesn't include European Castle or Tenchu, Incorporated.

UNLOCK TENCHU, INCORPORATED LEVEL IN MISSION EDITOR

At the Custom Missions Select screen, hold L2 and then press Circle, Square, Left, Right, Circle, Square.

COPY MISSIONS FROM CD IN MISSION EDITOR

At the Mission Settings Menu, hold Circle and then press Up, Up, Down, Down, Left, Right.

TEST DRIVE 6

Enter the following codes as a name:

CODE	NAME
$6,000,000	AKJGQ
All Cars	DFGY
All Tracks	ERERTH

All Tracks.

All Quick Race Tracks	CVCVBM
No Quick Race Tracks	OCVCVBM
Shorter Tracks	QTFHYF
All Challenges	OPIOP
No Challenges	OPOIOP
Disable Checkpoint	FFOEMIT
Enable Checkpoint	NOEMIT
Stop the Bomber Mode	RFGTR

TEST DRIVE LE MANS

CHEAT CODES

Enter the following as your name:

CODE	EFFECT
FIRSTON	Win the race
MAYOU	1999 Audi R8R
POHLIN	1999 BMW V12 LMR

1999 BMW V12 LMR.

PINOU	1999 Toyota GT-1
NAIMAR	Spacecraft race
BUGGYX	Replace X with a number

between 1 and 8 to race as one of eight buggies

Buggy.

CODE	EFFECT
HOTDOG	Race as Hotdog in a race against other foods
FROMAGE	Race as Cheese in a race against other foods
PIE	Race as PorkPie in a race against other foods

Race as PorkPie.

PIZZA	Race as Pizza in a race against other foods
MM1 or MM8	Race as Spacecraft in Motor Mash race
MM2	Race as Jet in Motor Mash race
MM3	Race as Mad in Motor Mash race
MM4	Race as Taxi in Motor Mash race
MM5	Race as Bus in Motor Mash race
MM6	Race as Ice in Motor Mash race
MM7	Race as Submarine in Motor Mash race

Race as Submarine.

JACKPOT	Hawaiian Tropic girl

TOMB RAIDER CHRONICLES

UNLIMITED AMMO AND MEDIKITS

Highlight the Small Medikit, hold L1 + L2 + R1 + R2 and press Up.

ALL KEYS AND ITEMS FOR CURRENT LEVEL

Highlight the Large Medikit, hold L1 + L2 + R1 + R2 and press Down.

ALL CUTSCENES

At the Main Menu, hold R2 and press Select.

TOMORROW NEVER DIES

INVINCIBILITY

Pause the game, and then press Select, Select, ●, ●, ▲, Select. The game will un-pause when entered correctly. To cancel the code, just re-enter it.

ALL WEAPONS, FULL AMMO, AND MED KITS

Pause the game, and then press Select, Select, ●, ●, L1, L1, R1, R1. The game will un-pause when entered correctly. To cancel the code, just re-enter it. This only gives you the weapons available in that mission.

DEBUG INFORMATION

Pause the game, and then press Select, Select, ●, ●, L2, R2, L2. The game will un-pause when entered correctly. To cancel the code, pause the game and press Select, Select, ●, ●, R2, L2, R2.

Debug Information.

TOGGLE HUD

Pause the game, and then press Select, Select, ●, ●, Left, Right, Select. The game will un-pause when entered correctly. To cancel the code, just re-enter it.

INVINCIBILITY AND NO CLIPPING

Pause the game, and then press Select, Select, ●, ●, ▲(X4). The game will un-pause when entered correctly. To cancel the code, just re-enter it.

Invincibility and No Clipping.

NO GROUND/SEE THROUGH SOME WALLS

Pause the game, and then press Select, Select, ●, ●, Select, Select, ●, ●. The game will un-pause when entered correctly. To cancel the code, just re-enter it.

CHEAT CAMERA

Pause the game, and then press Select, Select, ●, ●, R2, R2. The game will un-pause when entered correctly. To cancel the code, just re-enter it.

Cheat Camera.

WIN MISSION

Pause the game, and then press Select, Select, ●, ●, Select, ●. The game will un-pause when entered correctly. To cancel the code, just re-enter it.

Win Mission.

FREEZE OBJECTS

Pause the game, and then press Select, Select, ●, ●, Select, Select, R1, R1. The game will un-pause when entered correctly. To cancel the code, just re-enter it. This code does *not* freeze enemies, only objects.

LEVEL SELECT

At the Main Menu, and press Select, Select, ●, ●, L1, L1, ●, L1, L1. You will hear a sound when entered correctly.

VIEW MOVIES

At the Main Menu, and press Select, Select, ●, ●, L1(X7). You will hear a sound when entered correctly.

View Movies.

TONY HAWK'S PRO SKATER 2

HIDDEN CHARACTERS

At the Main Menu, hold L1 and press Up, Square, Square, Triangle, Right, Up, Circle, Triangle. This causes the wheel to spin. Then create a skater and give him the name of anyone on the Neversoft team. For example, name your skater Mick West and he'll appear. The best one is Connor Jewett, the son of Neversoft's President. (Don't change the appearance of the kid-sized skaters. It could crash your game.)

You must enter the following codes after pausing the game. While the game is paused, press and hold L1, and enter the codes.

FATTER SKATER

X (x4), Left, X (x4), Left, X (x4), Left

THINNER SKATER

X (x4), Square, X (x4), Square, X (x4), Square

TOGGLE BLOOD ON/OFF

Right, Up, Square, Triangle

STATS AT ALL 10S

X, Triangle, Circle, Square,
Triangle, Up, Down

SPECIAL METER
ALWAYS YELLOW

X, Triangle, Circle, Circle, Up, Left,
Triangle, Square

SUPER SPEED MODE

Down, Square, Triangle, Right, Up, Circle, Down, Square, Triangle, Right,
Up, Circle

UNLOCK EVERYTHING

X, X, X, Square, Triangle, Up, Down, Left, Up, Square, Triangle, X, Triangle,
Circle, X, Triangle, Circle

BIG HEAD

Square, Circle, Up, Left, Left,
Square, Right, Up, Left

80'S TONY

Complete 100% of the game with
Tony Hawk.

SPIDER-MAN

Complete 100% of the game with a custom skater.

CHEAT MENU

Complete 100% of the game with the rest of the skaters to open the following in order:

CHEAT	DESCRIPTION
Officer Dick	The first hidden character
Skip to restart	Pause the game and you can choose between starting points
Kid Mode	Increased stats, harder to bail tricks, kid-sized skaters
Perfect Balance	Never lose balance on grinds and manuals
Always Special	Special meter always full
STUD Cheat	Stats maxed out; It won't show in the Buy Stats screen, but it's there
Weight Cheat	Change weight of skater
Wireframe	Wireframe mode
Slow-Nic	Tricks in slow motion
Big Head Cheat	Big heads
Sim Mode	More realistic play
Smooth Cheat	No textures
Moon Physics	Bigger jumps
Disco Mode	Blinking lights
Level Flip	Levels are mirrored

PRIVATE CARRERA

Perform every gap in the game, except for Chopper Drop and Skater Heaven.

80'S TONY VIDEO

Earn three gold medals with McSqueeb (80's Tony). To view this video, start any competition, then End Run.

NEVERSOFT BAILS VIDEO

Earn three gold medals with Officer Dick.

SPIDER-MAN VIDEO

Earn three gold medals with Spider-Man

NEVERSOFT MAKES VIDEO

Earn three gold medals with Private Carrera

CHOPPER DROP: HAWAII LEVEL

Earn three gold medals with every skater.

SKATER HEAVEN

Complete 100% of the game with every skater, including secret characters.

GYMNASIUM IN SCHOOL LEVEL

Grind the Roll Call! Opunsezmee Rail with 1:40 on the clock to open the door to the gym.

TRIPLE PLAY 2001

EA DREAM TEAM

Select Single Game and press Left, Right six times at the Team Select screen. You should hear "Triple Play Baseball" when entered correctly.

EA Dream Team.

COMMENTARY

Hold L1 + L2 + R1 + R2 and enter the following. (**Note:** "Additional Batter Info" doesn't work with every batter.)

COMMENTARY	CODE
Historical	Up, ▲, Right, ●
Trivia	Down, X, Right, ●
Weather	X, Down, ▲, Up
Additional Batter Info	Left, ■, Up, ▲

URBAN CHAOS

ALL LEVELS

At the Main Menu, press R1 + L1 + Start + Select.

All Levels.

WCW MAYHEM

HIDDEN WRESTLERS UNLOCKED
Enter **PLYHDNGYS** as a Pay-Per-View password.

CLASSIC NITRO SETTING
Enter **PLYNTRCLSC** as a Pay-Per-View password.

IDENTICAL WRESTLERS IN 2-PLAYER VS MODE
Enter **DPLGNGRS** as a Pay-Per-View password.

MASKED REY MYSTERIO JR.
Enter **MSKDLTLRY** as a Pay-Per-View password.

QUEST CHEAT
Enter **CHT4DBST** as a Pay-Per-View password. Press Right in Quest for the Best to move up.

MOMENTUM METER
Enter **PRNTMMNTM** as a Pay-Per-View password.

TEST CASE 1 UNLOCKED (SPECIAL VERSION OF SOME WRESTLERS)
Enter **NGGDYNLN** as a Pay-Per-View password.

SPECIAL AREA SELECT ENABLED
Enter **CBCKRMS** as a Pay-Per-View password.

STAMINA METER
Enter **PRNTSTMN** as a Pay-Per-View password.

BIONIC CREATED WRESTLERS
Enter **MKSPRCWS** as a Pay-Per-View password.

X-MEN: MUTANT ACADEMY

UNLOCK EVERYTHING
At the Main Menu, press Select, Up, L2, R1, L1, R2. You will hear a sound when entered correctly. Press Select + Start to lock everything back.

THE GAMES

GAME NAME	PAGE
ARMY MEN: SARGE'S HEROS	96
CAPCOM VS. SNK	97
CENTIPEDE	102
CRAZY TAXI	102
DRACONUS: CULT OF THE WYRM	103
DYNAMITE COP	103
ESPN INTERNATIONAL TRACK AND FIELD	104
EXPENDABLE	104
F355 CHALLENGE	105
HIDDEN & DANGEROUS	106
HYDRO THUNDER	107
MAG FORCE RACING	107
MORTAL KOMBAT GOLD	108
MTV SPORTS: SKATEBOARDING	111
NBA 2K1	111
NFL BLITZ 2001	111
NFL QUARTERBACK CLUB 2000	115
PSYCHIC FORCE 2012	115
QUAKE III: ARENA	116
RAYMAN 2	117
READY 2 RUMBLE, ROUND 2	117
SAMBA DE AMIGO	118
SAN FRANCISCO RUSH 2049	118
SEGA BASS FISHING	120
SOUL CALIBUR	121
SPEED DEVILS	122
STREET FIGHTER ALPHA 3	122
SUPER RUNABOUT: SAN FRANCISCO EDITION	123
TNN MOTORSPORTS HARDCORE HEAT	123
TEST DRIVE 6	123
TONY HAWK'S PRO SKATER 2	124
TOY COMMANDER	126
TRICK STYLE	126
UTLIMATE FIGHTING CHAMPIONSHIP	128

WACKY RACES	128
WILD METAL	128
WWF ATTITUDE	129
ZOMBIE REVENGE	129

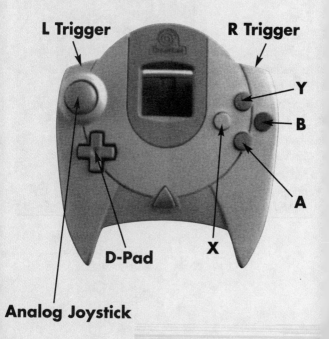

L Trigger

R Trigger

Y

B

A

X

D-Pad

Analog Joystick

ARMY MEN SARGE'S HEROES

PASSWORDS

LEVEL	PASSWORD
Attack	LNLGRMM
Spy Blue	TRGHTR
Bathroom	TDBWL
Riff Mission	MSTRMN
Forest	TLLTRS
Hoover Mission	SCRDCT
Thick Mission	STPDMN
Snow Mission	BLZZRD
Shrap Mission	SRFPNK
Fort Plastro	GNRLMN
Scorch Mission	HTTTRT
Showdown	ZBTSRL
Sandbox	HTKTTN
Kitchen	PTSPNS
Living Room	HXMSTR
The Way Home	VRCLN

CAPCOM VS. SNK

Secret Shop

NUMBER	NAME	COST	REQUIREMENTS	DESCRIPTION
1 - 33	Extra Colors	200 each	Select a character as a team member and clear Arcade Mode.	Hidden colors will appear in the Secret Shop.
34	Evil Ryu	7000	Select Ryu as a team member in Capcom Groove and clear Arcade Mode.	
35 - 48; 50 - 61	Extra Character	ratio 1: 2000 ratio 2: 3000 ratio 3: 4000	Select a character as a team member in their respective Groove and clear Arcade Mode.	EX characters are characters from previous versions of Capcom and SNK games.
49	Blood Iori	7000	Select Iori as a team member in SNK Groove and clear Arcade Mode.	
62	The Strongest Challenger	500	Clear Arcade Mode five times. Have over 85 Groove Points by the time your fifth battle is over while fighting the CPU to get The Strongest Challenger as the last boss.	If you're using Capcom Groove it will take place on Bison's stage, if you're using SNK Groove it will take place on Akuma's Stage.

97

NUMBER	NAME	COST	REQUIREMENTS	DESCRIPTION
63	Challenger from the Dark Realm	700	Defeat Arcade Mode with all 14 default Capcom characters. You must be using Capcom Groove and in your first three battles perform more than four Super Combo Finishes. Have over 60 Groove Points by the time your third battle is over while fighting the CPU and the Challenger from the Dark Realm will interrupt you.	
64	Messenger of Nature	700	Defeat Arcade Mode with all 14 default SNK characters. You must be using SNK Groove and in your first three battles perform more than four Super Combo Finishes. Have over 60 Groove Points by the time your third battle is over while fighting the CPU and The Messenger of Nature will interrupt you.	

NUMBER	NAME	COST	REQUIREMENTS	DESCRIPTION
65	M.Bison Stage	1000	Defeat M.Bison and clear the game in Arcade Mode.	
66	Geese Stage	1000	Defeat Geese and clear the game in Arcade Mode.	
67	Morrigan Stage	1200	Defeat Morrigan and clear the game in Arcade Mode.	
68	Nakoruru Stage	1200	Defeat Nakoruru and clear the game in Arcade Mode.	
69	Akuma Stage	1500	Defeat Akuma and clear the game in Arcade Mode.	
70	Secret Stage	1500	Clear Arcade Mode once after unlocking the Secret Stage. There is a 1 in 256 chance that you'll unlock the Secret Stage when facing Sagat in Arcade Mode. Each time you unlock an Extra Stage (65 through 69), those chances improve from 1/256, to 1/128, to 1/64, to 1/32, to 1/16.	

NUMBER	NAME	COST	REQUIREMENTS	DESCRIPTION
71	Pair Match Mode	1800	Defeat Morrigan and clear the game in Arcade Mode once. Defeat Nakoruru and clear the game in Arcade Mode once.	Changes all characters to Ratio 2, and allows selection of the same character more than once. Battles will always be 2 on 2. Exceptions: CPU Boss fight, CPU Nakoruru fight, CPU Morrigan fight.
72	Character Ratio Select	1500	Defeat CPU Akuma in Arcade Mode.	In VS Mode, allows you to select a Ratio of 1 to 4 for any character you choose. You can also select the same character more than once. Example: Ryu is normally a Ratio 2 character, but you will be able to change him to Ratio 1, 3, or even 4.
73	Original Theme Music	2000	Clear Pair Match Mode once.	
74	Player Character Morrigan	8000	Unlock all Extra Characters on the Capcom side, defeat Morrigan and clear the game in Arcade Mode.	Allows you to use Morrigan as a playable character in every mode.
75	Player Character Nakoruru	8000	Unlock all Extra Characters on the SNK side. Defeat Nakoruru and clear the game in Arcade Mode once.	Allows you to use Nakoruru as a playable character in every mode.

NUMBER	NAME	COST	REQUIREMENTS	DESCRIPTION
76	Player Character Akuma	9500	Meet all three requirements: Unlock Morrigan and Nakoruru as playable characters. Unlock the Original Theme Music. Defeat the CPU Akuma in Arcade Mode.	Allows you to use Akuma as a playable character in every mode.
77	Run & Dash	2300	Unlock Morrigan and Nakoruru as playable characters. Clear Pair Match Mode three times.	Allows you to turn Run and Dash systems on and off in the Option Mode.

A B C D E F G H I J K L M N O P Q R S T U V W X Y Z

CENTIPEDE

EXTRA LIVES AND ALL LEVELS

During a game, hold A + B + X + Y + L + R and rotate the Analog-Stick in either direction. You should get a message of "Get a Life" or "All Levels" if entered correctly.

CRAZY TAXI

TAXI BIKE

At the Character Select screen, press L Trigger + R Trigger (x3) and then hold L Trigger + R Trigger and press Up.

ANOTHER DAY

At the Character Select screen, hold R Trigger and press A to select your character. The phrase "Another Day" will appear on-screen.

NO ARROWS

Hold Start + R Trigger as the Character Select screen appears. The phrase "No Arrows" will appear on-screen.

NO DESTINATION MARK

Hold Start + L Trigger as the Character Select screen appears. The phrase "No Destination Mark" will appear on-screen.

EXPERT MODE(NO ARROWS OR DESTINATION MARK)

Hold L Trigger + R Trigger + Start as the Character Select screen appears. The word "EXPERT" will appear on-screen.

DIFFERENT VIEWS AND SPEEDOMETER

During a game, press the Start button on a controller in port three. You can then press A, B or Y on this controller to toggle between views. Press X (x5) for the speedometer. Press X again to turn off the speedometer.

DRACONUS: CULT OF THE WYRM

CHEAT MODE

At the title screen, press X, Y, Y, X, X, Y, Y. If entered correctly, you can now pause during a game, hold L + R and enter the following:

EFFECT	BUTTON PRESS
Full health	Right
Invincibility and 50,000 attacks	Left

DYNAMITE COP

TRANQUILIZER GUN MINI GAME

Complete the game.

BONUS MISSIONS

Complete missions 1, 2, and 3 to unlock missions 4, 5, and 6.

PLAY AS THE MONKEY

Complete missions 4, 5, and 6.

PLAY AS CINDY

Highlight **Ivy** at the Character Select screen and press Start.

PLAY AS ORIGINAL BRUNO FROM DIE HARD ARCADE

Collect all of the illustrations in the game.

ESPN INTERNATIONAL TRACK AND FIELD

ALL EVENTS

At the title screen, press Up, Up, Down, Down, Left, Right, Left, Right, B, A. You will hear a sound if entered correctly. This will open up Trap Shooting, Vault, Triple Jump and High Jump.

METALLIC ATHLETES

Select Trial Mode and enter the following names to get different colored metallic athletes.

ATHENS	SEOUL
ATLANTA	SYDNEY
HELSINKI	TOKYO
MEXICO	
MOSCOW	
MONTREAL	
MUNICH	
ROMA	

EXPENDABLE

LEVEL SELECT

Pause the game and press Up, Down, Up, Down, Up, Down, Left, Right, Right, Y.

LEVEL SKIP

Pause the game and press Y, Y, X, X, L, R, Down, Down, Up, Up.

EXTRA LIVES

Pause the game and press A, B, X, Y, L Trigger, R Trigger, Up, Down, Left, Right.

EXTRA CREDITS

Pause the game and press A, B, Left, A, B, Right, B, A, Down, R Trigger.

GRENADES

Pause the game and press Down (x5), Up (x4), R Trigger.

SHIELDS

Pause the game and press Up, Down, Left, Right, X, Up, Down, Left, Right, Y.

INSTANT VICTORY

Pause the game and press L Trigger, R Trigger, L Trigger, R Trigger, Left, Right, Left, Right, Y, X.

1ST PERSON VIEW

Pause the game and press L Trigger, Left, R Trigger, Right, X, X, Down, Down, R Trigger, L Trigger.

F355 CHALLENGE

HIDDEN COURSES

Hold X + Y at the Options screen to access the passwords option. These passwords are case-sensitive. Enter the following to access the hidden tracks:

PASSWORD	COURSE
DaysofThunder	Atlanta
LiebeFrauMilch	Nurburgring
Stars&Stripes	Laguna-Seca
KualaLumpur	Sepang
CinqueValvole	Fiorano

HIDDEN & DANGEROUS

ENABLE CHEATS

Enter your name as IWILLCHEAT. Now you can enter the following with a keyboard, while paused (unless noted):

EFFECT	CHEAT
All Items	ALLLOOT
Open Doors (in current mission)	OPENALLDOOR
Skip Mission	MISSIONOVER
Fail Mission	GAMEFAIL
Full Health	GOODHEALTH
Invincibility	CANTDIE
Kill Enemies	KILLTHEMALL
Resurrect Teammates	RESURRECTION
Coordinates	PLAYERCOORDS
Big Heads	FUNNYHEAD (at the team setup screen)
Alternate Uniforms	LARACROFT
Wireframe	DEBUGDRAWWIRE
Behind Enemy Camera	ENEMYB
Front Enemy Camera	ENEMYF
Uncensored German Version	BLUESTARS
Ending (this will end your game)	SHOWTHEEND

CHEAT MODE

When putting in your name, enter RVL, keep a second L highlighted and press Start. Press B to go back to the main menu. ALL MISSIONS should now be below the menu. Pause during gameplay to get more cheats.

HYDRO THUNDER

MEDIUM DIFFICULTY TRACKS AND BOATS

Complete the three Easy difficulty tracks in first, second, or third.

HARD DIFFICULTY TRACKS AND BOATS

Complete the Medium difficulty tracks in first or second place.

BONUS TRACKS AND TINY-TANIC

Complete the Medium difficulty tracks in first place to unlock the first bonus course. Complete this bonus course in first place to unlock the next bonus course and so on. There are four bonus tracks and boats. After you unlock the bonus tracks, you can race with the Tiny-tanic.

FISHING BOAT

After unlocking all of the hidden tracks, highlight the Thresher at the Boat Select screen, press and hold L Trigger + R Trigger, and press Y, Y. Select the Chumdinger to race in a fishing boat.

ALL TRACKS IN 2-PLAYER MODE

Race each track in 2-Player mode and win.

TURBO START

To get a four-second boost at the start of the race, do the following (you will hear "Super Start" when done correctly):

1. Hold the Left Trigger while the game loads.

2. Release the Left Trigger and hold the Right Trigger as the "3" fades.

3. Release the Right and hold the Left as the "2" fades.

4. Release the Left and hold the Right as the "1" fades.

MAG FORCE RACING

ALL TRACKS AND TRIPODS

At the main menu, highlight Tripod Select. Hold X + Y and press Up, Left, Down, Right, Right, Up, Down, Right.

JOHN MALKOVICH

Enter the code JOHNM.

TRIPLE MISSILES

Enter the code MISSI.

TURBO RAMS

Enter the code TURBO.

TURBO RAM AUTO PILOT

Enter the code AUTOM.

INVISIBLE TRIPODS

Enter the code GHOST

ALTERNATE SOUNDS

Enter the code RETRO.

MORTAL KOMBAT GOLD

CHEAT MENU

At the Title screen, press Up, Up, Down, Down, Left, Left, Right, Right. You will hear a laugh and the word "Outstanding" when entered correctly. Then highlight Options at the Main Menu and hold Block + Run. This will give you a Cheat Menu with the following options:

Easy Endings: A character's ending will play after one round.

Fatal 1 (HP): Press **HP** to perform fatality 1.

Fatal 2 (LP): Press **LP** to perform fatality 2.

Pit Fatal (D + HP): Press **Down** + **HP** to perform the Pit fatality.

Danger: Sets life bars to one hit deaths.

Kombat Kode: (1-30): Allows the following cheats in 2-player mode:

0: Default

1: Big Head Mode

2: Disable Throws

3: Disable Maximum Damage

4: Disable Maximum Damage & Throws

5: Unlimited Run

6: Free Weapon

7: Random Weapons

8: Armed & Dangerous

9: Many Weapons

10: Silent Kombat

11: Explosive Kombat

12: No Power/Danger

13: Default Kombat

14: Weapon Kombat

15: Noob Saibot Mode

16: Red Rain

17: Goro's Lair

18: The Well

19: Elder Gods

20: Tomb

21: Wind World

22: Reptile's Lair

23: Shaolin Temple

24: Living Forrest

25: Prison

26: Ice Pit

27: Church

28: Netherealm

29: Soul Chamber

30: Ladder

FIGHT AS GORO

Enable the Cheat Menu code. Highlight Hidden on the Character Select screen, and hold L Trigger + R Trigger and press Up, Left, A.

FIGHT AS SEKTOR

Enable the Cheat Menu code. Highlight Hidden on the Character Select screen, and hold L Trigger + R Trigger and press Up (x4), Left (x4), A.

FIGHT AS NOOB SAIBOT

Enable the Cheat Menu code. Highlight Hidden on the Character Select screen, and hold L Trigger + R Trigger and press Up, Up, Left (x4), A.

ACCESS MEAT

Keep choosing Group in a 2-player game. After winning with all the characters, select any character. You will be that character, but with a different look. This is Meat, and all his moves are dependent upon which character you choose.

CHARACTER BIOGRAPHIES

Select Kombat Theater, highlight a character, and press L Trigger + R Trigger.

ALTERNATE COSTUMES

At the Character Select screen, highlight a character, hold Start, and press any button.

KOMBAT KODES

Enter the following codes at the Versus screen. Player One enters the first three digits, where Low Punch is the first button, Block is the second, and Low Kick is the third. Player Two enters the second set of three numbers in the same manner.

EFFECT	CODE
Unlimited Run	001 001
No Power	123 123
Noob Saibot Mode	012 012
Red Rain (Rain stage only)	020 020
Explosive Kombat	050 050
All Time Weapons	002 002
Disable Throws	100 100
Disable Max Damage	010 010
No Throws & Max Damage	110 110
Free Weapon	111 111
Random Weapon	222 222
Armed & Dangerous	444 444
Many Weapons	555 555
Silent Kombat	666 666
Big Heads	321 321
Goro's Lair	011 011
The Well	022 022

EFFECT	CODE
The Elder God's Stage	033 033
The Tomb	044 044
Wind World	055 055
Reptile's Lair	066 066
Shaolin Temple	101 101
Living Forest	202 202
The Prison	303 303
Soul Chamber	353 353
The Church	323 323
Ladder Stage	363 363
The Netherealm	343 343
Ice Pit	313 313

MTV SPORTS: SKATEBOARDING

UNLOCK BOARDS, PARKS, COSTUMES AND SKATERS

Enter PASWRD as a name at the lifestyle screen.

NBA 2K1

SEGANET, MO CAP AND SEGA SPORTS TEAMS

Select Codes from the Options menu and enter vc.

NFL BLITZ 2001

VS CHEATS

Go to the versus screen and press Turbo, Jump and Passto change the icons below the helmets. Once the code is enetered press the d-pad or analog stick in the direction indicated. The code name will appear with a sound if entered correctly. Example to do Infinite turbo press Turbo (5 times), Jump, Pass (4 times) and press the stick Up.

EFFECT	CODE
Tournament mode	1-1-1 Down
Infinite turbo	5-1-4 Up

EFFECT	CODE
Fast turbo running	0-3-2 Left
Power-up offense	3-1-2 Up
Power-up defense	4-2-1 Up
Power-up teammates	2-3-3 Up
Power-up blockers	3-1-2 Left
Super blitzing	0-4-5 Up
Super field goals	1-2-3 Left

Invisible	4-3-3 Up
No random fumbles	4-2-3 Down
No first downs	2-1-0 Up
No interceptions	3-4-4 Up
No punting	1-5-1 Up
Allow stepping out of bounds	2-1-1 Left
Fast passes	2-5-0 Left
Late hits	0-1-0 Up
Show field goal %	0-0-1 Down
Hide receiver name	1-0-2 Right
Big football	0-5-0 Right
No head	3-2-1 Left
Headless team	1-2-3 Right

EFFECT	CODE
Show more field (2 Player Agreement)	0-2-1 Right
No CPU assistance (2 Player Agreement)	0-1-2 Down
Powerup speed (2 Player Agreement)	4-0-4 Left
Hyper blitz (2 Player Agreement)	5-5-5 Up
No play selection (2 Player Agreement)	1-1-5 Left
Smart CPU opponent (1 Player Game)	3-1-4 Down
Always quarterback (2 Human Players on same team)	2-2-2 Left
Weather: snowy	5-2-5 Down

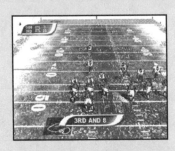

Weather: rain	5-5-5 Right
No Hiliting On Target Receiver	3-2-1 Down
Deranged blitz mode (In A 1 Player Game)	2-1-2 Down
Ultra hard mode (In A 1 Player Game)	3-2-3 Up
Jason Loves Mystery Ball	3-2-3 Left

Unlimited throws	2-2-3 Right
Super passing mode	4-2-3 Right

TEAM PLAYBOOKS

EFFECT	CODE
Arizona Cardinals	1-0-1 Left
Atlanta Falcons	1-0-2 Left
Baltimore Ravens	1-0-3 Left
Buffalo Bills	1-0-4 Left
Carolina Panthers	1-0-5 Left
Chicago Bears	1-1-0 Left
Cincinnati Bengals	1-1-2 Left
Cleveland Browns	1-1-3 Left
Dallas Cowboys	1-1-4 Left
Denver Broncos	1-1-5 Right
Detroit Lions	1-2-1 Left
Green Bay Packers	1-2-2 Left
Indianapolis Colts	1-2-3 Up
Jacksonville Jaguars	1-2-4 Left
Kansas City Chiefs	1-2-5 Left
Miami Dolphins	1-3-1 Left
Minnesota Vikings	1-3-2 Left
New England Patriots	1-3-3 Left
New Orleans Saints	1-3-4 Left
New York Giants	1-3-5 Left
New York Jets	1-4-1 Left
Oakland Raiders	1-4-2 Left
Philadelphia Eagles	1-4-3 Left
Pittsburgh Steelers	1-4-4 Left
San Diego Chargers	1-4-5 Left
San Francisco 49ers	1-5-1 Left
Seattle Seahawks	1-5-2 Left
St. Louis Rams	1-5-3 Left
Tampa Bay Buccaneers	1-5-4 Left
Tennessee Titans	1-5-5 Left
Washington Redskins	2-0-1 Left

NFL QUARTERBACK CLUB 2000

Enter the following at the cheat screen:

EFFECT	CODE
More Injuries	HSPTL
Alien Stadium	SCLLYMLDR
Rugby Play	RGBY
Flubber Ball	FLBBR
Short Players	SHRTGYS
More Fumbles	BTTRFNGRS
Slow Motion	FRRSTGMP
Get Obese Players	MRSHMLLW
Get Thin Players	TTHPCK
Big Coin at Coin Toss	BGMNY
Double Downs	DBLDWNS
Huge FootBall	BCHBLL
Landmine Mode	PPCRNRTRNS
Players on Fire	HSNFR

PSYCHIC FORCE 2012

FIGHT AS RICHARD WONG

Accumulate over six hours of gameplay, or complete Story mode with all 10 characters.

FIGHT AS KEITH EVANS

Accumulate over 12 hours of gameplay, or unlock Uon and complete Arcade Mode with all of the characters.

FIGHT AS BURN GLIFFIS

Accumulate over 14 hours of gameplay, or unlock Uon and Kiss and complete Story Mode and Arcade Mode with all of the characters.

EVIL SILVER EMILIO

Accumulate over 16 hours of gameplay, or fight as Emilio 30 times. You can select this by pressing the X button.

A B C D E F G H I J K L M N O P Q R S T U V W X Y Z

GOOD GOLDEN EMILIO

Accumulate over 18 hours of gameplay, or fight as Emilio 50 times. You can select this by pressing the Y button.

HIDDEN STAGES (VS MODE)

Access the following stages after unlocking the corresponding character:

STAGE	CHARACTER
Palace	Richard Wong
Noa	Keith Evans
Midnight	Burn Gliffis
Psychic Zone	Silver Emilio

QUAKE III ARENA

CONSOLE COMMANDS

You will need the keyboard and mouse to perform these commands. While in the game hit ~ to access the game console. Now you can enter the following commands:

COMMAND	EFFECT
/who	List of players
/help	Display the list of commands
/say	Type a message to everyone
/say1	Message to Player 1
/say2	Message to Player 2
/say3	Message to Player 3
/say4	Message to Player 4
/say_team	Message to team
/tell_attacker	Message to attacker
/tell_target	Message to target
/clear	Clear console

RAYMAN 2: THE GREAT ESCAPE

GLOBOX DISC ACCESS GAME

At the title screen, press Start, then hold L + R and press B, B, B, B before the screen scrolls all the way down.

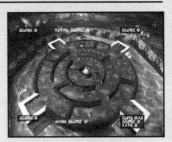

READY 2 RUMBLE BOXING ROUND 2

HAPPY HOLIDAYS!

On each Holiday (Halloween, Christmas, New Years, July 4th, Easter, etc.) the game does a holiday theme, based on the internal clock. For example, on Halloween the ring turns orange and black and J.R. Flurry wears a skeleton costume. Change your clock and you can see all the Holiday themes!

Fun Codes

Big Gloves mode	←→↑↓, R, L
Chubby mode	→→↑↓→, R, R, L
Toothpick mode	→→↑↓→, R, L
Zombie mode	←↑→↓, R, R, L

RUMBLING RING

Select Afro Thunder. Before the fight begins, press A, X, A, A, B, Y and the screen will shake!

CHAMPIONSHIP OUTFITS

Finish the game once in Championship Mode.

117

UNLOCK SECRET CHARACTERS

Beat Arcade Mode to unlock these secret characters in the following order:

Freak E. Deke	Freedom Brock
Michael Jackson	Rocket Samchay
G.C. Thunder	Mr. President
Wild "Stubby" Corley	The First Lady
Shaquille O'Neal	

Rumbleman

Defeat Arcade Mode on the Hardest difficulty to open Rumbleman.

SAMBA DE AMIGO

ALL MUSIC MODE

Select arcade mode, then quickly shake Left Maraca High fifteen times at the height selection screen to unlock all songs. Note: For the standard Dreamcast controller, hold the Left Maraca High button.

RANDOM MODE

Quickly shake Left Maraca Low fifteen times at the difficulty selection screen. Note: For the standard Dreamcast controller, hold the Left Maraca Low button.

SUPER HARD MODE

Quickly shake Left Maraca High fifteen times at the difficulty selection screen. Note: For the standard Dreamcast controller, hold the Left Maraca High button.

SAN FRANCISCO RUSH 2049

CHEAT MENU

At the main menu highlight Options and press L + R + X + Y.

ALL CARS

At the Cheat Menu, highlight All Cars and press A, A, Y, Y, L, L. Then hold R + X, release, and hold L + A.

TRACK ORIENTATION

At the Cheat Menu, highlight Track Orientation, hold L + R and press X. Release and press A, X, Y. Then hold L + R and press X.

SUPER SPEED

At the Cheat Menu, highlight Super speed, hold Y + R and press L. Release, and press A + X, A, A, A.

INVINCIBLE

At the Cheat Menu, highlight Invincible, hold L + X, press Y, A then release and hold R + A + X + Y.

INVISIBLE CAR

At the Cheat menu, highlight Invisible Car and press L + X, R + Y, A. Hold L + R and press X. Release and press Y, Y, Y.

INVISIBLE TRACK

At the Cheat Menu, highlight Invisible Track, and press R, L, Y, X, A, A, X, Y. Then, hold L + R and press A.

BRAKES

At the Cheat Menu, highlight Brakes and press Y, Y, Y, L + R + A + X.

FOG COLOR

At the Cheat Menu, highlight Fog color. Hold L + X, release, then hold A + X and release. Hold Y + X, release and hold R + X.

SUPER TIRES

At the Cheat Menu, highlight Super Tires, hold R and press X, X, X. Release R, hold L and press A, A, Y.

MASS

At the Cheat Menu, highlight Mass, hold A and press X, X, Y. Release A and press L, R.

DEMOLITION BATTLE

At the Cheat Menu, highlight Demolition Battle, hold L + A and press Y, X. Release, hold R + A and press Y, X.

RANDOM WEAPONS

At the Cheat Menu, highlight Random Weapons, hold L + A and press X, Y. Then, hold R + A and press X, Y.

B
C
D
E
F
G
H
I
J
K
L
M
N
O
P
Q
R
S
T
U
V
W
X
Y
Z

INTERMEDIATE CIRCUIT

Get 3rd Place or better in Beginner Circuit.

7.0 LITER V8

Total at least 800 miles.

DISCO STUNT TRACK

Get 100,000 points in Stunt Mode.

OASIS STUNT TRACK

Get 250,000 points in Stunt Mode.

WAREHOUSE STUNT TRACK

Get 500,000 points in Stunt Mode.

OBSTACLE COURSE

Get 1 million points in Stunt Mode.

VENOM VEHICLE

Get all silver coins in Stunt Mode.

GX2 CAR

Get half the gold coins in Stunt Mode.

EXTREME CIRCUIT AND PRESIDIO TRACK

Get 3rd Place or better in Intermediate Circuit.

LX CAR

Get 24 gold coins in Stunt Mode.

BATTLE MODE DOWNTOWN TRACK

Get 100 kills in Battle Mode.

BATTLE MODE PLAZA TRACK

Get 250 kills in Battle Mode.

BATTLE MODE ROADKILL TRACK

Get 500 kills in Battle Mode.

BATTLE MODE FACTORY TRACK

Get 1000 Kills in Battle Mode.

SEGA BASS FISHING

FEMALE CHARACTER

After selecting Arcade Mode, press A + B at the Level Select screen.

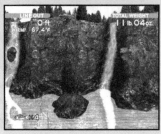

BONUS PRACTICE LEVELS

Complete Amateur Tournament in Original Mode to unlock the Falls. Complete Challenge Tournament in Original Mode to unlock Palace.

SONIC LURE

Complete Professional Tournament in Original Mode.

SOUL CALIBUR

BONUS CHARACTERS AND STAGES

Complete Arcade Mode with each of the original characters to unlock a new character or stage in the following order:

Hwang	Siegfried Stage
Yoshimitsu	Rock
Lizard Man	Rock Stage
Yoshimitsu Stage	Seung Mina
Siegfried	Cervantes

EDGE MASTER

Complete Arcade Mode with all 17 characters.

INFERNO

After unlocking Edge Master, complete Arcade Mode with Xianghua using her third costume. The easiest way to get her third costume is to earn 130 points in Mission Mode and purchasing pictures 002, 006, 015 and 039.

ALTERNATE OUTFITS

Each character has at least two outfits. Press Y to select the second outfit. The following characters have a third outfit: Siegfried, Xianghua, Sophitia, Maxi, and Voldo. You must earn each of these outfits in Mission Mode, except for Siegfried, who already has his. Once you have the third outfit, select it by holding Y and pressing A or X.

SPEED DEVILS

ALL CARS AND TRACKS

During gameplay, press B, Right, B, Right, Up, B, Up.

SKIP CURRENT CLASS

During a gameplay, press Down, Right, Down, Right, A, X, A.

INFINITE NITROS

During a gameplay, press Down, Up, Down, Up, A, X, A.

EXTRA MONEY

During a gameplay, press A, Right, A, Right, Up, B, A.

STREET FIGHTER ALPHA 3

PLAY AS SUPER AKUMA

At the Character Select screen, highlight Akuma, hold Start, and press A.

PLAY AS SUPER M.BISON

At the Character Select screen, highlight M.Bison, hold Start and press A.

SUPER RUNABOUT: SAN FRANCISCO EDITION

ALL CARS AND LEVELS

Enter Elvis!!! as your name.

TNN MOTORSPORTS HARDCORE HEAT

BEELZEBUB BUGGY

Successfully complete Expert Mode in first place.

JET BUGGY

Achieve 100 percent on the level checker when building your car.

ADDITIONAL EXPERT RACES

Successfully complete Expert Mode under the Championship difficulty using the Beelzebub Buggy.

ADDITIONAL COLOR SCHEME

Successfully complete Expert Mode.

TEST DRIVE 6

CHEATS

Enter name as the following:

NAME	EFFECT
AKJGQ	$6,000,000

A B C D E F G H I J K L M N O P Q R S T U V W X Y Z

NAME	EFFECT
ERERTH	All tracks in Practice and Single Race
DFGY	All cars in Practice Mode

| RFGTR | Unlocks Stop the Bomber |

TONY HAWK'S PRO SKATER 2

TOGGLE BLOOD

Pause the game, hold L Trigger and press Right, Up, X, Y.

STATS AT ALL 10S

Pause the game, hold L Trigger and press A, Y, B, X, Y, Up, Down.

SPECIAL METER ALWAYS FULL

Pause the game, hold L Trigger and press A, Y, B, B, Up, Left, Y, X.

25% FASTER

Pause the game, hold L Trigger and press Down, X, Y, Right, Up, B, Down, X, Y, Right, Up, B.

80'S TONY

Complete 100% of the game with Tony Hawk.

SPIDER-MAN

Complete 100% of the game with a custom skater.

CHEAT MENU

Complete 100% of the game with the rest of the skaters to open the following in order:

CHEAT	DESCRIPTION
Officer Dick	The first hidden character
Skip to restart	Pause the game and you can choose between starting points

CHEAT	DESCRIPTION
Kid Mode	Increased stats, harder to bail tricks, kid-sized skaters
Perfect Balance	Never lose balance on grinds and manuals
Always Special	Special meter always full
STUD Cheat	Stats maxed out; It won't show in the Buy Stats screen, but it's there
Weight Cheat	Change weight of skater
Wireframe	Wireframe mode
Slow-Nic	Tricks in slow motion
Big Head Cheat	Big heads
Sim Mode	More realistic play
Smooth Cheat	No textures
Moon Physics	Bigger jumps
Disco Mode	Blinking lights
Level Flip	Levels are mirrored

PRIVATE CARRERA

Perform every gap in the game, except for Chopper Drop and Skater Heaven.

80'S TONY VIDEO

Earn three gold medals with McSqueeb (80's Tony). To view this video, start any competition, then End Run.

NEVERSOFT BAILS VIDEO

Earn three gold medals with Officer Dick.

SPIDER-MAN VIDEO

Earn three gold medals with Spider-Man

NEVERSOFT MAKES VIDEO

Earn three gold medals with Private Carrera

CHOPPER DROP: HAWAII LEVEL

Earn three gold medals with every skater.

SKATER HEAVEN

Complete 100% of the game with every skater, including secret characters.

GYMNASIUM IN SCHOOL LEVEL

Grind the Roll Call! Opunsezmee Rail with 1:40 on the clock to open the door to the gym.

TOY COMMANDER

ALL MAPS

Pause the game, then hold the L Trigger and press A, Y, X, B, Y, X. You will hear music when entered correctly.

HEAVY WEAPON

Pause the game, then hold the L Trigger and press X, A, Y, B, A, X. You will hear music when entered correctly.

SWITCH MACHINE GUN

Pause the game, then hold the L Trigger and press B, A, Y, X, A, B. You will hear music when entered correctly.

99 HEAVY AMMUNITION

Pause the game, then hold the L Trigger and press A, B, X, Y, B, A. You will hear music when entered correctly.

FIX TOY

Pause the game, then hold the L Trigger and press A, X, B, Y, A, Y. You will hear music when entered correctly.

TRICK STYLE

You can disable the following cheats by accessing the Cheats menu and selecting the code. You then get an option to Disable Cheat.

WIN EVERYTHING

Select Cheats from the Options and enter **citybeacons**. This enables you to play any race.

ALWAYS WIN

Select Cheats from the Options and enter **tearound**. You will win even if you don't finish first.

INFINITE TIME

Select Cheats from the Options and enter **iwish**. This gives you no time limits when racing.

POWER-UP MOVES

Select Cheats from the Options and enter **travolta**. This enables you to do moves that would normally require a power-up.

BIG HEADS

Select Cheats from the Options and enter **inflatedego**.

COMBAT BOARD

Defeat the Boss on the U.K. track.

TURBO BOARD

Defeat the Boss on the U.S. track.

STUNT BOARD

Defeat the Boss on the Japan track.

QUICK START

When "Go" appears on-screen, hold R Trigger.

ULTIMATE FIGHTING CHAMPIONSHIP

999 SKILL POINTS IN CAREER MODE

Enter "Best" as the first name and "Buy" as the last.

WACKY RACES

For the following codes, you will find the Cheats option on the sign just behind where you begin. After entering the code go to Code Collection to turn it on.

ALL ABILITIES

Enter BARGAINBASEMENT as a code.

ALL CARS

Enter WACKYSPOILERS as a code.

ALL CHALLENGES AND TRACKS

Enter WACKYGIVEAWAY as a code.

SUPER DIFFICULT MODE

Enter CRACKEDNAILS as a code.

WILD METAL

INVINCIBILITY

Press Y, Right, B, Left, X, Down during game play.

ALL WEAPONS

Press A(2), Right, Y, A, Right during game play.

FULL HEALTH

Press Down(2), A, X, B, X during game play.

LEVEL SKIP

Press Up, Right, B, Y, Down, Left during game play.

SPEED BOOST

Press Up, X, Down, B, A, Y during game play.

FRIENDLY AI UNITS

Press B, Down, A, Down, X, Y during game play.

REVEAL ALL TOKEN LOCATIONS

Press Y, B, A, Left, Down, Down during game play.

WWF ATTITUDE

CAREER MODE BONUSES

Defeat the following titles and events in Career Mode to unlock the corresponding bonuses:

TITLE OR EVENT	BONUSES
European Title	Sable, Marc Mero, Trainer, squeaky mode, new custom stuff
Intercontinental Title	Jaqueline, Chyna, big head mode, three additiono! attribute points
WWF Heavyweight Title	Head, beep mode, ego mode
King of the Ring PPV	Kurrgan, Taka Michinoku
SummerSlam PPV	Sgt. Slaughter, Shawn Michaels.
Royal Rumble PPV	Jerry Lawler, Paul Bearer.

ZOMBIE REVENGE

ALTERNATE OUTFITS

As you select a character, hold Start and press B, X, or Y.

STAGE SELECT IN FIGHTING MODE

After selecting Fighting Mode, hold Start while selecting 1P vs CPU, 1P vs 2P or CPU vs CPU.

THE GAMES

GAME NAME	PAGE
A BUG'S LIFE	132
ALL STAR BASEBALL 2001	132
ARMORINES IN PROJECT S.W.A.R.M.	133
ARMY MEN: AIR COMBAT	134
ARMY MEN: SARGE'S HEROES	135
ARMY MEN: SARGE'S HEROES 2	136
BATTLETANX: GLOBAL ASSAULT	137
BATTLEZONE: RISE OF THE BLACK DOGS	137
CRUIS'N WORLD	138
CYBERTIGER WOODS GOLF	139
DESTRUCTION DERBY 64	140
DUKE NUKEM: ZERO HOUR	140
EXCITEBIKE 64	143
GOLDENEYE 007	145
HOT WHEELS TURBO RACING	159
INTERNATIONAL TRACK AND FIELD 2000	161
JEREMY MCGRATH SUPERCROSS 2000	162
KNOCKOUT KINGS 2000	162
MADDEN NFL 2000	163
MARIO GOLF	165
MARIO TENNIS	166
MONSTER TRUCK MADNESS 64	168
NBA COURTSIDE 2: FEATURING KOBE BRYANT	171
NBA SHOWTIME	174
THE NEW TETRIS	177
NFL BLITZ 2001	178
PAPERBOY	179
PERFECT DARK	181
QUAKE 2	187
RAINBOW SIX	189
ROADSTERS	190
SAN FRANCISCO RUSH 2049	191
SUPERCROSS 2000	192

GAME NAME	PAGE
TOP GEAR RALLY 2	193
WINBACK: COVERT OPERATIONS	194
XENA: WARRIOR PRINCESS, THE TALISMAN OF FATE	194

N64® LEGEND

ABBREV.	WHAT IT MEANS
L Button	Left Shift button on top of controller
R Button	Right Shift button on top of controller
Left	Left on control pad
Right	Right on control pad
Up	Up on control pad
Down	Down on control pad
A	A button on control pad
B	B button on control pad
Z	Z trigger
CU	"Up" C button on control pad
CR	"Right" C button on control pad
CD	"Down" C button on control pad
CL	"Left" C button on control pad

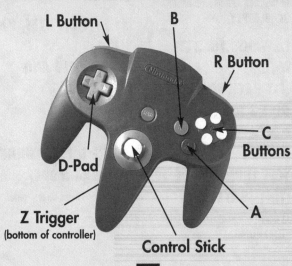

L Button

B

R Button

C Buttons

D-Pad

A

Z Trigger
(bottom of controller)

Control Stick

A BUG'S LIFE

LEVEL SELECT

At the Main Menu, hold Z + C-Left + C-Right + C-Up + C-Down and press the R Button. Move to the right past the Anthill to access the other levels.

Level Select.

ALL STAR BASEBALL 2001

BALL TRAIL MODE

At the Enter Cheats screen, enter **WLDWLDWST**.

BIG BALL MODE

At the Enter Cheats screen, enter **BCHBLKTPTY**.

I...WANT...TO...FLY AWAY
(FLY BACK TO DUGOUT DOING THE WORM)

At the Enter Cheats screen, enter **FLYAWAY**.

TOM THUMB MODE
(TINY PLAYERS)

At the Enter Cheats screen, enter **TOMTHUMB**.

AREN'T THESE THINGS ILLEGAL?
(HARDER HITS)

At the Enter Cheats screen, enter **HOLLOWBATS**.

MY EYES MY EYES, I'M BLIND
(WHITE FIELD AND STADIUM))

At the Enter Cheats screen, enter **MYEYES**.

WHERE'D EVERYTHING GO (DARK MODE)

At the Enter Cheats screen, enter **WTOTL**.

ARMORINES IN PROJECT S.W.A.R.M.

For the following codes, select the Cheat Option and enter the appropriate code:

CODE	ENTER
All Missions	SKIPPY (You must start a new game to select a mission.)

Invincibility	GODLY
All Weapons	LOADED
Unlock All Cheats	GOLDENPIE
Unlimited Ammunition	SORTED
Fast Run	SONIC
Pen and Ink Mode	SKETCHY

CODE	ENTER
Egypt Worker Bug (Multiplayer Mode)	CLAW
Female Trooper (Multiplayer Mode)	GODDESS
Volcano Guard Bug (Multiplayer Mode)	RUBBER
Hive Worker Bug (Multiplayer Mode)	UGLY
Hive Guard Bug (Multiplayer Mode)	LEGGY

A B C D E F G H I J K L M N O P Q R S T U V W X Y Z

MISSION PASSWORDS

Enter the following as passwords:

MISSION	PASSWORD
2	PNTNNP
3	NGMLQP
4	SPLGZW
5	DQRFKW
6	PSQQLW
7	NBGJVX
8	VKPDMX
9	SDKNSX
10	PVBWGJ
11	NWVCHJ

ARMY MEN: AIR COMBAT

1-PLAYER CAMPAIGN PASSWORDS

MISSION	CODE
2	Up, Down, Left, Right
3	Up, Down, Left, Up
4	Down, Up, Left, Right
5	Down, Up, Left, Down
6	Down, Up, Right, Down
7	Left, Down, L Button, Up
8	Left, Down, L Button, Down
9	Left, Up, L Button, Down
10	L Button, Up, Left, Down
11	L Button, Up, Left, Up
12	L Button, Up, L button, Down
13	L Button, Down, Up, Left
14	R Button, C-Left, Up, Right
15	C-Down, L Button, Down, Down
16	R Button, C-Left, Right, Up

ARMY MEN: SARGE'S HEROES

To access the following codes, enter the following as passwords:

CODE	PASSWORD
All Weapons	NSRLS

All Weapons.

Maximum Ammunition	MMLVSRM
Test Information	THDTST
Mini Mode	DRVLLVSMM
Play as Tin Soldier	TNSLDRS
Play as Vikki	GRNGRLRX
Play as Plastro	PLSTRLVSVG

PASSWORDS

LEVEL	PASSWORD
Spy Blue	TRGHTR
Bathroom	TDBWL
Riff Mission	MSTRMN
Forest	TLLTRS
Hoover Mission	SCRDCT
Thick Mission	STPDMN
Snow Mission	BLZZRD
Shrap Mission	SRFPNK
Fort Plastro	GNRLMN
Scorch Mission	HTTTRT
Showdown	ZBTSRL

continued

A B C D E F G H I J K L M N O P Q R S T U V W X Y Z

LEVEL	PASSWORD
Sandbox	HTKTTN
Kitchen	PTSPNS
Living Room	HXMSTR
The Way Home	VRCLN

ARMY MEN: SARGE'S HEROES 2

LEVEL PASSWORDS

LEVEL	PASSWORD
2 Bridge	Fllngdwn
3 Fridge	Gtmlk
4 Freezer	Chllbb
5 Inside Wall	Clsngn
6 Graveyard	Dgths
8 Tan Base	Bdbz
9 Revenge	Lbbck
10 Desk	Dskjb
11 Bed	Gtslp
12 Town	Smllvll
13 Cashier	Chrgt
14 Train	Ntbrt
15 Rockets	Rdglr
16 Pool	Fstnls
17 Pinball	Whswzrd

TIN SOLDIER

Enter the code TNMN.

BATTLETANX: GLOBAL ASSAULT

LEVEL SELECT
Enter **80DYS** as a code.

INVINCIBILITY
Enter **HPPYHPPY** as a code.

ALL WEAPONS
Enter **RCKTSRDGLTR** as a code.

Level Select.

CAMPAIGN MODE BONUS LEVEL
Enter **WRDRB** as a code. This unlocks a secret level after you've completed Campaign Mode.

CUSTOM 1 GANG
Enter **TRDDYBRRKS** as a code

BRANDON GAME
Enter **NNKNHCKS** as a code.

BATTLEZONE: RISE OF THE BLACK DOGS

FREE BUILDINGS
At the Main menu, hold Z and press A, B, A, B.

FREE SATELLITE
At the Main menu, hold Z and press B, C-Left, C-Down, A.

INFINITE AMMO
At the Main menu, hold Z and press L Button, R Button, L Button, R Button.

INFINITE ARMOR
At the Main menu, hold Z and press Up, Right, Down, Left.

A B C D E F G H I J K L M N O P Q R S T U V W X Y Z

UNLOCK ALL LEVELS

At the Main menu, hold Z and press C-Up, C-Right, C-Down, C-Left, Start.

CRUIS'N WORLD

HIDDEN CARS

In Practice Championship mode, beat the indicated times at each track to open the car:

ON THIS TRACK	BEAT THIS TIME	GET THIS CAR
Australia	1:49	Surgeon
China	1:14	Enforcer
Egypt	1:07	Skool Bus
England	1:46	Bulldog
France	2:15	Tommy
Germany	2:27	New York Taxi
Hawaii	3:47	Monsta
Japan	2:48	Rocket
Kenya	2:06	Conductor
Mexico	1:46	Howler
New York	2:11	Grass Hopper
Russia	1.58	Rocket

SPEED DEMON CAR

Get all the points in Champion Mode.

CYBERTIGER WOODS GOLF

PLAY AS LILTIGER

Select Tiger, choose Edit Name, and change it to **Prodigy**.

PLAY AS MARVIN THE ALIEN

Select any character, choose Edit Name, and change it to **Ufo**.

PLAY AS KIMMI

Select any character, choose Edit Name, and change it to **Rapper**.

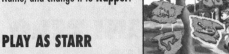

PLAY AS STARR

Select any character, choose Edit Name, and change it to **Retro**.

UNLOCK VOLCANO COURSE

Select any character, choose Edit Name, and change it to **Sthelens**.

A B C D E F G H I J K L M N O P Q R S T U V W X Y Z

DESTRUCTION DERBY 64

BONUS CARS

To earn additional bonus cars, you must win the World Championships.

Bonus Cars.

CIRCUIT	BONUS CAR
Novice	Street Rocket
Amateur	Taxi
Professional	Pickup Truck
Legend	Ambulance

DUKE NUKEM: ZERO HOUR

CHEAT MENU

At the Press Start screen, press Down, Down, A, Z, Z, Left, A. You'll hear a tone when entered correctly.

Cheat Menu.

1ST PERSON PERSPECTIVE

At the Press Start screen, press Down, Up, L Button, B, Z, Left, C-Up, C-Right, C-Left, Z. You'll hear a tone when entered correctly.

FREEZE THROWER WITH UNLIMITED AMMO

At the Press Start screen, press Down, Up, A, L Button, R Button, Z. You'll hear a tone when entered correctly.

UNLIMITED RIFLE AMMO

At the Press Start screen, press C-Up, C-Down, C-Left, C-Right, L Button, R Button. You'll hear a tone when entered correctly.

CHARACTER SET 1

At the Press Start screen, press A, L Button, R Button, Left, B, Down, Up. You'll hear a tone when entered correctly.

Character Set 1.

CHARACTER SET 2

At the Press Start screen, press B, A, A, R Button, L Button. You'll hear a tone when entered correctly.

CHARACTER SET 3

At the Press Start screen, press L Button, L Button, Up, Down, R Button, B, A. You'll hear a tone when entered correctly.

Character Set 3.

CHARACTER SET 4

At the Press Start screen, press B (x3), R Button, Left, A. You'll hear a tone when entered correctly.

CHARACTER SET 5

At the Press Start screen, press Right, B, Left, L Button, A, Z. You'll hear a tone when entered correctly.

CHARACTER SET 6

At the Press Start screen, press Up, Down, B, A, A, Left. You'll hear a tone when entered correctly.

Character Set 6.

BIG HEAD MODE

Rescue all the babes in Level 2: Liberty or Death.

BIG GUN MODE

Defeat all the enemies in Level 3: Nuclear Winter.

SECRET LEVEL: WETWORLD

After powering up at the end of Level 3: Nuclear Winter, jump onto the roof below. From the roof, jump into the water and swim to the floating platform.

FLAT SHADE MAP

You must uncover all the secrets in the secret level, Wetworld.

ICE SKINS

You must rescue all the babes in Level 5: Fallout.

WEATHER

Obtain all the secrets in Level 6: Under Siege.

FAST ZOMBIES

You must rescue all the babes in Level 8: Dry Town.

MAXIMUM BLASTER AMMO

Defeat all the enemies in Level 9: Jailbreak.

MAXIMUM SHOTGUN AMMO

Rescue all the babes in Level 10: Up Ship Creek.

MAXIMUM RIFLE AMMO

Rescue all the babes in Level 11: Fort Roswell.

MAXIMUM REVOLVER AMMO

Rescue all the babes and obtain all the secrets in Level 12: Probing the Depths.

MAXIMUM SAWED-OFF SHOTGUN AMMO

Defeat all the enemies in Level 13: The Whitechapel Killings.

MAXIMUM SMG AMMO

Obtain all the secrets in Level 15: Dawn of the Duke.

MAXIMUM GATTLING GUN AMMO

Defeat all the enemies in Level 16: Hydrogen Bomb.

MAXIMUM VOLT-C AMMO

Obtain all the secrets in Level 17: The Rack.

SECRET LEVEL: GOING DOWN

Obtain all of the time machine pieces before reaching the rack. A second portal should appear in a room adjacent to the first.

MAXIMUM SNIPER AMMO

Rescue all babes in the secret level, "Going Down".

MAXIMUM FREEZER AMMO

Defeat all the enemies in Level 20: The Brothers Nukem.

MAXIMUM GAMMA AMMO

Rescue all the babes in Level 21: Alien Mothership.

EXCITEBIKE 64

ACCESS THE ENTER A CHEAT CODE SCREEN

At the Main menu, hold L Button + C Right + C Down + A.

Enter A Cheat Code

Mirror Mode Enabled
Press the A Button

YADAYADA

BIG HEAD MODE

Enter **BLAHBLAH** as a cheat code.

SMALL HEAD MODE

Enter **PINHEAD** as a cheat code.

BEAT THIS!!

Enter **PATWELLS** as a cheat code.

STUNT BONUS

Enter **SHOWOFF** as a cheat code.

INVISIBLE RIDER

Enter **INVISRIDER** as a cheat code.

MIRROR MODE

Enter **YADAYADA** as a cheat code.

NIGHT MODE

Enter **MIDNIGHT** as a cheat code.

ALL STUNTS

Enter **TRICKSTER** as a cheat code.

UNLOCK HILL CLIMB

Finish 1st in the Gold Round of the Amateur Season.

3D EXCITEBIKE

Finish 1st in the Challenge Round of the Pro Season.

UNLOCK ORIGINAL EXCITEBIKE

Finish the Tutorial Mode.

UNLOCK SOCCER

Finish 1st in the Silver Round of the Novice Season.

GOLDENEYE 007

CHEAT MENU

You can earn the cheats by completing the levels under a certain time limit. Here are the easy ways to get the cheats. You can enter the following during gameplay.

INVINCIBILITY

1. Hold the L Button and press Down
2. Hold the R Button and press C-Right
3. Hold the R Button and press C-Up
4. Hold the L Button and press Right
5. Hold the L Button and press C-Down
6. Hold the R Button and press C-Up
7. Hold the L Button and press Right
8. Hold the R Button and press Down
9. Hold the L Button and press Left
10. Hold the L Button + the R-Button and press C-Right

ALL GUNS

1. Hold the L Button + the R-Button and press Down
2. Hold the L Button and press C-Left
3. Hold the L Button and press C-Right
4. Hold the L Button + the R-Button and press C-Left
5. Hold the L Button and press Down
6. Hold the L Button and press C-Down
7. Hold the R Button and press C-Left
8. Hold the L Button + the R-Button and press C-Right
9. Hold the R Button and press Up
10. Hold the L Button and press C-Left

MAXIMUM AMMUNITION

1. Hold the L Button + the R-Button and press C-Right
2. Hold the R Button and press Up
3. Hold the R Button and press Down
4. Hold the R Button and press Down
5. Hold the L Button + the R-Button and press C-Right
6. Hold the L Button + the R-Button and press Left
7. Hold the R Button and press Down

continued

A B C D E F G H I J K L M N O P Q R S T U V W X Y Z

8. Hold the R Button and press Up
9. Hold the L Button + the R-Button and press C-Right
10. Hold the R Button and press Left

LINE MODE

1. Hold the R Button and press C-Down
2. Hold the L Button + the R-Button and press Down
3. Hold the L Button and press Right
4. Hold the R Button and press C-Up
5. Hold the L Button + the R-Button and press C-Right
6. Hold the R Button and press Up
7. Hold the L Button and press Down
8. Hold the L Button and press Right
9. Hold the R Button and press C-Left
10. Hold the R Button and press C-Up

INVISIBILITY

1. Hold the R Button and press C-Left
2. Hold the L Button + the R-Button and press C-Up
3. Hold the L Button + the R-Button and press Left
4. Hold the L Button + the R-Button and press Up
5. Hold the R Button and press Up
6. Hold the L Button and press C-Left
7. Hold the R Button and press C-Up
8. Hold the L Button and press C-Down
9. Hold the L Button + the R-Button and press Left
10. Hold the R Button and press Right

INVISIBILITY IN MULTIPLAYER

1. Hold the L Button and press C-Up
2. Hold the L Button + the R-Button and press C-Left
3. Hold the R Button and press Up
4. Hold the L Button and press C-Right
5. Hold the R Button and press C-Left
6. Hold the L Button and press Right
7. Hold the L Button + the R-Button and press C-Left
8. Hold the L Button and press C-Right
9. Hold the L Button and press Up
10. Hold the L Button + the R-Button and press C-Down

The following codes must be entered at the Mission Select Screen:

UNLOCK FACILITY

1. Hold the L Button + the R-Button and press C-Up
2. Hold the R Button and press C-Left
3. Hold the L Button and press Left
4. Hold the R Button and press C-Up
5. Hold the L Button and press Left
6. Hold the R Button and press C-Down
7. Hold the L Button and press C-Right
8. Hold the R Button and press Right
9. Hold the L Button + the R-Button and press C-Up
10. Hold the L Button and press Right

UNLOCK RUNWAY

1. Hold the L Button + the R-Button and press Left
2. Hold the R Button and press Left
3. Hold the L Button and press C-Up
4. Hold the L Button and press Left
5. Hold the R Button and press C-Up
6. Hold the R Button and press C-Down
7. R Button +C-Right
8. Hold the R Button and press Right
9. Hold the L Button and press Down
10. Hold the R Button and press C-Left

UNLOCK SURFACE I

1. Hold the R Button and press C-Left
2. Hold the L Button + the R-Button and press C-Up
3. Hold the L Button and press Left
4. Hold the R Button and press Up
5. Hold the R Button and press Left
6. Hold the L Button and press Up
7. Hold the R Button and press C-Down
8. Hold the L Button and press Right
9. L Button +C-Right
10. Hold the L Button + the R-Button and press Down

A B C D E F G H I J K L M N O P Q R S T U V W X Y Z

UNLOCK BUNKER I

1. Hold the L Button and press C-Down
2. Hold the R Button and press Right
3. Hold the L Button and press C-Right
4. Hold the R Button and press C-Left
5. Hold the L Button and press C-Down
6. Hold the L Button + the R-Button and press Left
7. Hold the L Button and press C-Right
8. Hold the L Button + the R-Button and press Up
9. Hold the R Button and press C-Right
10. Hold the L Button and press Up

UNLOCK SILO

1. Hold the L Button and press Up
2. Hold the R Button and press C-Down
3. Hold the L Button and press Left
4. Hold the R Button and press Down
5. Hold the L Button and press C-Left
6. Hold the L Button + the R-Button and press C-Right
7. Hold the L Button and press C-Up
8. Hold the R Button and press Right
9. Hold the R Button and press Right
10. R Button +C-Right

UNLOCK FRIGATE

1. Hold the R Button and press C-Up
2. Hold the L Button and press Down
3. Hold the R Button and press C-Right
4. Hold the L Button and press Left
5. Hold the L Button + the R-Button and press Up
6. Hold the L Button + the R-Button and press C-Down
7. Hold the R Button and press C-Right
8. Hold the R Button and press Up
9. Hold the L Button + the R-Button and press C-Down
10. Hold the R Button and press Up

UNLOCK SURFACE 2

1. Hold the L Button and press C-Down
2. Hold the L Button + the R-Button and press C-Right
3. Hold the R Button and press C-Right
4. Hold the R Button and press C-Up
5. Hold the R Button and press C-Left
6. Hold the L Button and press Right
7. Hold the L Button + the R-Button and press C-Up
8. Hold the L Button and press C-Up
9. Hold the L Button + the R-Button and press Down
10. Hold the L Button and press C-Right

UNLOCK BUNKER 2

1. Hold the L Button and press Down
2. Hold the R Button and press Down
3. Hold the L Button + the R-Button and press C-Up
4. Hold the L Button and press Left
5. Hold the L Button + the R-Button and press Right
6. Hold the L Button and press C-Left
7. Hold the R Button and press Right
8. Hold the L Button and press C-Up
9. Hold the L Button and press Left
10. Hold the L Button and press C-Down

UNLOCK STATUE

1. Hold the L Button + the R-Button and press C-Down
2. Hold the L Button + the R-Button and press C-Down
3. Hold the L Button and press Right
4. Hold the L Button + the R-Button and press Left
5. Hold the R Button and press Left
6. Hold the R Button and press C-Right
7. Hold the L Button + the R-Button and press Left
8. Hold the R Button and press C-Up
9. Hold the R Button and press C-Down
10. Hold the R Button and press Right

UNLOCK ARCHIVES

1. Hold the R Button and press Left
2. Hold the L Button + the R-Button and press Up
3. Hold the L Button + the R-Button and press C-Down
4. Hold the R Button and press Left
5. Hold the L Button + the R-Button and press C-Right
6. Hold the L Button and press Left
7. Hold the L Button + the R-Button and press Right
8. Hold the L Button + the R-Button and press C-Down
9. Hold the L Button and press Up
10. Hold the R Button and press C-Down

UNLOCK STREETS

1. Hold the L Button + the R-Button and press C-Left
2. Hold the L Button and press C-Right
3. Hold the L Button and press Up
4. Hold the L Button + the R-Button and press C-Down
5. Hold the R Button and press C-Right
6. Hold the R Button and press C-Down
7. Hold the R Button and press Left
8. Hold the R Button and press C-Down
9. Hold the R Button and press C-Up
10. Hold the L Button and press Down

UNLOCK DEPOT

1. Hold the L Button and press Down
2. Hold the L Button and press Down
3. Hold the R Button and press C-Down
4. Hold the L Button and press C-Right
5. Hold the L Button + the R-Button and press Right
6. Hold the R Button and press C-Left
7. Hold the L Button and press Down
8. Hold the L Button and press C-Left
9. Hold the L Button and press C-Right
10. Hold the L Button and press Up

UNLOCK TRAIN

1. Hold the R Button and press Left
2. Hold the R Button and press C-Down
3. Hold the R Button and press C-Right
4. Hold the L Button + the R-Button and press Left
5. Hold the L Button and press Right
6. Hold the R Button and press C-Down
7. Hold the L Button and press Left
8. Hold the L Button + the R-Button and press C-Left
9. Hold the L Button and press Up
10. Hold the L Button and press C-Up

UNLOCK JUNGLE

1. Hold the R Button and press C-Down
2. Hold the R Button and press Left
3. Hold the L Button + the R-Button and press Up
4. Hold the R Button and press Right
5. Hold the R Button and press Down
6. Hold the R Button and press Down
7. Hold the R Button and press Up
8. Hold the R Button and press C-Left
9. Hold the R Button and press C-Up
10. Hold the L Button + the R-Button and press Left

UNLOCK CONTROL CENTER

1. Hold the L Button and press C-Down
2. Hold the R Button and press Down
3. Hold the L Button and press Right
4. Hold the R Button and press C-Right
5. Hold the R Button and press C-Down
6. Hold the R Button and press Left
7. Hold the R Button and press Left
8. Hold the R Button and press C-Up
9. Hold the R Button and press Left
10. Hold the L Button + the R-Button and press C-Up

UNLOCK CAVERNS

1. Hold the L Button and press Down
2. Hold the R Button and press C-Down

continued

3. Hold the L Button + the R-Button and press Up
4. Hold the L Button and press Right
5. Hold the R Button and press C-Up
6. Hold the R Button and press C-Left
7. Hold the R Button and press Up
8. Hold the L Button and press C-Left
9. Hold the L Button and press Up
10. Hold the R Button and press C-Left

UNLOCK CRADLE

1. Hold the L Button + the R-Button and press C-Up
2. Hold the L Button and press Left
3. Hold the R Button and press Down
4. Hold the L Button and press Down
5. Hold the L Button and press C-Up
6. Hold the L Button and press Down
7. Hold the R Button and press Right
8. Hold the R Button and press C-Up
9. Hold the L Button and press C-Left
10. Hold the R Button and press Right

You must enter the following at the Cheat Menu. You should hear a beep when entered correctly. Exit the Cheat Menu and re-enter to access the cheat.

ACTIVATE PAINTBALL CHEAT

1. Hold the L Button and press Up
2. Press C-Up
3. Hold the R Button and press Right
4. Hold the L Button + the R-Button and press C-Left
5. Hold the L Button and press Up
6. Hold the R Button and press C-Down
7. Hold the L Button and press C-Down
8. Hold the L Button + the R-Button and press C-Down
9. Hold the L Button + the R-Button and press Up
10. Hold the L Button and press C-Down

ACTIVATE INVINCIBILITY CHEAT

1. Hold the R Button and press Left
2. Hold the L Button and press Down
3. Press Left
4. Press Up
5. Press Down
6. Hold the R Button and press C-Left
7. Hold the L Button and press C-Left
8. Hold the L Button + the R-Button and press Left
9. Hold the L Button + the R-Button and press Right
10. Hold the L Button and press C-Left

ACTIVATE DK MODE CHEAT

1. Hold the L Button + the R-Button and press Up
2. C-Right
3. Hold the R Button and press Left
4. Hold the R Button and press Up
5. Up
6. Hold the R Button and press Right
7. Up
8. Hold the L Button + the R-Button and press C-Down
9. Hold the L Button + the R-Button and press Down
10. Hold the L Button and press R + C-Left

ACTIVATE 2X GRENADE LAUNCHER CHEAT

1. Hold the R Button and press Down
2. Hold the R Button and press Up
3. Press Right
4. Hold the L Button + the R-Button and press C-Down
5. Hold the L Button and press Right
6. Hold the R Button and press Left
7. Press Left
8. Press Down
9. Press Up
10. Hold the R Button and press C-Down

ACTIVATE 2X ROCKET LAUNCHER CHEAT

1. Hold the R Button and press Right
2. Hold the L Button and press Up

continued

3. Press Down
4. Press Down
5. Hold the R Button and press C-Down
6. Hold the L Button and press Left
7. Hold the L Button and press C-Left
8. Hold the R Button and press Up
9. Hold the R Button and press Down
10. Hold the R Button and press C-Left

ACTIVATE TURBO MODE CHEAT

1. Hold the L Button and press Down
2. Hold the L Button and press C-Down
3. Hold the L Button + the R-Button and press Up
4. Hold the R Button and press C-Down
5. Press Left
6. Hold the R Button and press Down
7. Hold the L Button and press C-Down
8. Press Up
9. Hold the R Button and press Down
10. Hold the L Button and press Right

ACTIVATE NO RADAR CHEAT [MULTIPLAYER]

1. Hold the R Button and press Up
2. Press C-Down
3. Press C-Left
4. Press C-Up
5. Hold the L Button and press Down
6. Hold the R Button and press Up
7. Press C-Left
8. Press Right
9. Hold the R Button and press Left
10. Hold the R Button and press Right

ACTIVATE NO RADAR CHEAT [MULTIPLAYER]

1. Hold the R Button and press Up
2. Press C-Down
3. Press C-Left
4. Press C-Up
5. Hold the L Button and press Down
6. Hold the R Button and press Up

continued

7. Press C-Left
8. Press Right
9. Hold the R Button and press Left
10. Hold the R Button and press Right

ACTIVATE TINY BOND CHEAT

1. Hold the L Button + the R-Button and press Down
2. Hold the R Button and press Down
3. Hold the L Button and press C-Down
4. Press Left
5. Hold the R Button and press C-Left
6. Hold the L Button + the R-Button and press C-Down
7. Press Right
8. Press Down
9. Hold the R Button and press C-Down
10. Hold the R Button and press Right

ACTIVATE 2X THROWING KNIVES CHEAT

1. Hold the R Button and press C-Left
2. Hold the L Button and press Left
3. Press Up
4. Hold the L Button + the R-Button and press Right
5. Press Right
6. Hold the L Button + the R-Button and press C-Left
7. Hold the L Button + the R-Button and press C-Left
8. Hold the R Button and press Down
9. Hold the R Button and press Left
10. Hold the R Button and press C-Left

ACTIVATE FAST ANIMATION CHEAT

1. Hold the L Button and press C-Down
2. Hold the L Button and press C-Left
3. Press C-Down
4. Press C-Right
5. Press C-Left
6. Hold the L Button + the R Button and press Right
7. C-Right
8. Hold the L Button + the R Button and press Up
9. R Button +C-Left
10. L Button +Left

A B C D E F G H I J K L M N O P Q R S T U V W X Y Z

ACTIVATE BOND INVISIBLE CHEAT

1. Hold the L Button + the R-Button and press C-Left
2. Hold the L Button + the R-Button and press C-Down
3. Hold the L Button and press C-Left
4. Hold the R Button and press C-Left
5. Hold the R Button and press Right
6. Hold the L Button + the R-Button and press Left
7. Hold the L Button and press Right
8. Press Left
9. Hold the L Button + the R-Button and press C-Left
10. Hold the L Button and press Down

ACTIVATE ENEMY ROCKETS CHEAT

1. Hold the L Button + the R-Button and press C-Down
2. Press C-Left
3. Hold the R Button and press C-Down
4. C-Down
5. Press C-Down
6. Hold the L Button + the R-Button and press C-Down
7. Hold the L Button + the R-Button and press Up
8. Press C-Down
9. Hold the R Button and press Up
10. Press the L Button +Up

ACTIVATE SLOW ANIMATION CHEAT

1. Hold the L Button + the R-Button and press Left
2. Hold the L Button + the R-Button and press Left
3 .Hold the L Button + the R-Button and press Down
4. Hold the L Button + the R-Button and press Left
5. Press C-Right
6. Hold the L Button and press the R Button and press Down
7. Hold the L Button + the R-Button and press Down
8. Hold the L Button and press Down
9. Press C-Left
10. Press C-Up

ACTIVATE SILVER PP7 CHEAT

1. Hold the L Button and press Left
2. Hold the L Button + the R-Button and press Up
3. Hold the L Button and press Right
4. Hold the L Button + the R-Button and press Up
5. Hold the L Button + the R-Button and press C-Left
6. Hold the L Button + the R-Button and press Left
7. Hold the L Button + the R-Button and press Down
8. Press C-Down
9. Hold the L Button + the R-Button and press Right
10. Hold the L Button + the R-Button and press Left

ACTIVATE 2X HUNTING KNIVES CHEAT

1. Hold the R Button and press C-Down
2. Hold the L Button and press Right
3. Hold the R Button and press C-Left
4. Hold the R Button and press Right
5. Hold the L Button and press the R Button and press Right
6. Hold the L Button + the R-Button and press Up
7. Hold the L Button and press Down
8. Hold the R Button and press Left
9. Hold the L Button and press Right
10. Hold the L Button and press C-Left

ACTIVATE INFINITE AMMO CHEAT

1. Hold the L Button and press C-Left
2. Hold the L Button + the R-Button and press Right
3. Press C-Right
4. Press C-Left
5. Hold the R Button and press Left
6. Hold the L Button and press C-Down
7. Hold the L Button and press the R Button and press Left
8. Hold the L Button and press the R Button and press C-Down
9. Press L Button +Up
10. Press C-Right

ACTIVATE 2X RCP-90S CHEAT

1. Press Up
2. Press Right

continued

3. Hold the L Button and press Left
4. Hold the R Button and press Down
5. Hold the L Button and press Up
6. Hold the L Button and press C-Left
7. Hold the L Button and press Left
8. Press C-Right
9. Press C-Up
10. Hold the L Button + the R-Button and press Down

ACTIVATE GOLD PP7 CHEAT

1. Hold the L Button + the R-Button and press Right
2. Hold the L Button + the R-Button and press Down
3. Hold the L Button and press Up
4. Hold the L Button + the R-Button and press Down
5. Press C-Up
6. Hold the R Button and press Up
7. Hold the L Button + the R-Button and press Right
8. Hold the L Button and press Left
9. Press Down
10. Hold the L Button and press C-Down

ACTIVATE 2X LASERS CHEAT

1. Hold the L Button and press Right
2. Hold the L Button + the R-Button and press C-Left
3. Hold the L Button and press Down
4. Hold the R Button and press Left
5. Hold the R Button and press Down
6. Hold the L Button and press Right
7. Press C-Up
8. Press Right
9. Hold the R Button and press Right
10. Hold the L Button + the R-Button and press Up

ACTIVATE ALL GUNS CHEAT

1. Press Down
2. Press Left
3. Press C-Up
4. Press Right
5. Press L Button +Down

6. Press L Button +Left
7. Press L Button +Up
8. Press C-Left
9. Press Left
10. Press C-Down

HOT WHEELS TURBO RACING

TRANSPARENT SURROUNDINGS

At the Main Menu, press C-Up, Z, C-Down, C-Left, C-Up, Z, C-Down, C-Left.

UNLIMITED TURBOS

At the Main Menu, press C-Right, Z, C-Up, C-Down, R Button, C-Left, Z, C-Right.

Transparent Surroundings.

RACE AT NIGHT

At the Main Menu, press C-Up, C-Up, C-Down, C-Down, C-Left, C-Right, C-Left, C-Right.

Race at Night.

MIRRORED TRACKS

At the Main Menu, press Z, R Button, Z, Z, R Button, Z.

TRANSPARENT CARS

At the Main Menu, press C-Left, Z, Z, C-Up, C-Left, R Button, C-Down, C-Up.

Transparent Cars.

TOW-JAM CAR

At the Main Menu, press C-Up, C-Down, Z, R Button, C-Left, C-Right, C-Up, C-Down.

Tow-Jam Car.

INTERNATIONAL TRACK AND FIELD 2000

ALL EVENTS

At the title screen, press Up, Up, Down, Down, Left, Right, Left, Right, B, A. You will hear a sound if entered correctly.

METALLIC ATHLETES

Select Trial Mode and enter the following names to get different colored metallic athletes. Names are case sensitive.

Athens

Atlanta

Helsinki

Mexico

Moscow

Munich

Roma

Seoul

Sydney

Tokyo

JEREMY MCGRATH SUPERCROSS 2000

CHEAT MODE

At the main menu, press L Button, C-Up, L Button, C-Up, L Button, C-Down, C-Up, C-Down.

KNOCKOUT KINGS 2000

BIG GLOVES

Pause the game and press C-Up, C-Down, C-Up, C-Up, C-Down. You will hear a bell when entered correctly. To turn off the code, enter it again.

BIG HEAD MODE

Pause the game and press C-Left, C-Right, C-Left, C-Left, C-Right. You will hear a bell when entered correctly. To turn off the code, enter it again.

Big Head Mode.

TALLER BOXER MODE

Pause the game and press C-Up, C-Down, C-Up, C-Up.

MADDEN NFL 2000

Enter the following at the Secret Code screen:

CODE	ENTER
All 60s Team	MOJO
All 70s Team	SIDEBURNS
All 80s Team	REAGANOMICS
All Madden Team	TEAMMADDEN
EA Sports Team	WEARETHEGAME
Industrials Team	INTHEFUTURE
Marshalls Team	COWBOYS

Marshalls Team.

Clown Team	SCARYCLOWN
Tiburon Team	SHARKATTACK

Tiburon Team.

Dodge City Stadium	WILDWEST
Christmas Stadium	XMASGIFT

A B C D E F G H I J K L M N O P Q R S T U V W X Y Z

Christmas Stadium.

CODE	ENTER
Circus Stadium	3RING
EA Sports Stadium	ITSINTHEGAME
Large Team Vs. Small Team	MICEANDMEN
Alternate Scoring	DRBENWAY
Curved Space and Time	EMC2
More Injuries	PAINFUL
Faster Fatigue	CHAINSMOKER
Floating Heads	GUILLOTINE

Floating Heads.

Perfect Passes	QBINTHECLUB
100 Yard Passes	PIGSKINSFLY
More Interceptions	PICKEDOFF
More Fumbles	ROLLERJAM
Fewer Penalties	REFISBLIND

MARIO GOLF

BONUS COURSES

At the Main Menu, highlight the Clubhouse option and press Z + R Button + A. Then enter the following:

CHEAT	CODE
Camp Hyrule, Cup 1	0EQ561G2
Camp Hyrule, Cup 2	5VW68906
Second Camp Hyrule Cup	5VW68906
Nintendo Power Tournament	KPXWN9N3

MARIO STAR COURSE

Open up the first five courses and get 2,200 points.

LEFT-HANDED GOLFER

Press Z or the L Button while selecting a character.

PLAY AS LUIGI

Defeat Luigi in the Get Character Mode.

PLAY AS YOSHI

After accessing Luigi, defeat Yoshi in the Get Character Mode.

PLAY AS SONNY

After accessing Luigi and Yoshi, defeat Sonny in the Get Character Mode.

PLAY AS WARIO

After accessing Luigi, Yoshi and Sonny, defeat Wario in the Get Character Mode.

PLAY AS HARRY

After accessing Luigi, Yoshi, Sonny, and Wario, defeat Harry in the Get Character Mode.

PLAY AS MARIO

After accessing Luigi, Yoshi, Sonny, Wario and Harry, defeat Mario in the Get Character Mode.

A B C D E F G H I J K L M N O P Q R S T U V W X Y Z

PLAY AS BOWSER

After accessing Luigi, Yoshi, Sonny, Wario, Harry and Mario, defeat Bowser in the Get Character Mode.

PLAY AS MAPLE

Earn 50 Birdie Badges in Tournament Mode.

PLAY AS METAL MARIO

Earn 108 Birdie Badges in Tournament Mode.

PLAY AS DONKEY KONG

Earn 30 points in Ring Mode.

MARIO TENNIS

PLAY LEFT-HANDED

Press Z or the L Button while selecting a character.

STAR CHARACTERS

Win the Star Cup with a character to access the star version of that character. Hold the R Button while you select your character.

SPECIAL GAMES

Select Special Games and then Ring Tournament. Enter the following codes to access these special Cups:

CUP	CODE
Bowser Cup	N24K8QN2P
Donkey Kong Cup	MM55MQMMJ
IGN64 Cup	V2UFMPUZM
Luigi Cup	M1C2YQM1W
Mario Cup	A3W5KQA3C
MarioTennis.com Cup	48HWOR482
Nintendo Power Cup	J6M9PQJ6U
Peach Cup	OF9XFQOFR
Blockbuster Cup	ARM6JQARU
Waluigi Cup	LA98JRLAR
Wario Cup	UOUFMPUOM

SHY GUY

Use anybody to win the singles Star Cup.

DONKEY KONG JR.

Use anybody to win the doubles Star Cup.

SUPER MARIO BROS. COURT

Use Mario to win the singles Mushroom Cup.

MARIO AND LUIGI COURT

Use Mario to win the doubles Star Cup.

BABY MARIO AND YOSHI COURT

Use Yoshi to win the singlesMushroom Cup.

DONKEY KONG COURT

Use Donkey Kong to win the singles Mushroom Cup.

BIRDO AND YOSHI COURT

Use Birdo to win the doubles Star Cup.

WARIO AND WALUIGI COURT

Use Wario to win the doubles Star Cup.

PIRANHA COURT

Win the Piranha Challenge by getting a perfect 50. You can only use this court in the Piranha Challenge.

A B C D E F G H I J K L M N O P Q R S T U V W X Y Z

MONSTER TRUCK MADNESS 64

LOW-RIDER TRUCKS

Enter **YRDR** as a password.

Low-Rider Trucks.

NEW FACIAL TEXTURE

Enter **JMPNG** as a password.

New Facial Texture.

BEGINNER PASSWORDS

COURSE	PASSWORD
Ruins	GO★NJ2L0
Junk Yard	J★XQYN4G
The Heights	M★0T1Q9RO
Voodoo Island	PO3W4TC★OFO
Greenhill Pass	5O627WFX9O23G
Wasteland	VO92O 2O0CL56B5V
Aztec Valley	YYC5D2L3FB89D8BB7

INTERMEDIATE PASSWORDS

COURSE	PASSWORD
Ruins	GBGJ5MTL
Junk Yard	JNJMQL7S
The Heights	MJMPT◐XRN
Voodoo Island	PJPSWR0★89R
Greenhill Pass	SBSV2★3XBC◐4♥
Wasteland	VBVY2X60♥FD7B2M
Aztec Valley	YFY15093H◐G♥◐5675
Alpine Challenge	1N1483C6KLJDH89◐G4N

EXPERT PASSWORDS

COURSE	PASSWORD
Ruins	GKGH◐G★◐
Junk Yard	JGJKLJP★
The Heights	MSMN◐M7QW
Voodoo Island	PKPQRP◐T793
Greenhill Pass	SKST★SDW◐C61R
Wasteland	VOVWXVGZDF9463R
Aztec Valley	YGY209YJ2G◐C796462
Alpine Challenge	101231M5JLF◐C979S0D
Death Trap	404564P8MBCDFCACV32KC

LEGENDARY DRIVERS

Select the listed track, highlight Select Car, and enter the following codes:

DRIVER	TRACK	CODE
Alan Kulwicki	Bristol	Left Shift, Right Shift, C-Up, C-Up, C-Down, C-Down, C-Left, C-Left, C-Right, C-Right

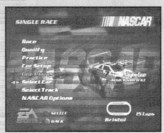

Alan Kulwicki.

DRIVER	TRACK	CODE
Benny Parsons	Richmond	Right Shift, Right Shift, Z, Z, Left Shift, Left Shift, C-Up, C-Up, C-Down, C-Down
Cale Yarborough	Darlington	C-Up, C-Left, C-Down, C-Right, C-Up, C-Left, C-Down, C-Right, Z, Z

Cale Yarborough.

Davey Allison	Talladega	C-Up, C-Down, C-Left, C-Right, C-Up, C-Down, C-Left, C-Right, Z, Z
Bobby Allison	Charlotte	C-Up, C-Right, C-Down, C-Left, C-Down, C-Right, C-Up, C-Right, Left Shift, Right Shift
David Pearson	Martinsville	Left Shift, Z, Right Shift, C-Right, C-Down, C-Left, C-Up, C-Right, Z, Z

NBA COURTSIDE 2: FEATURING KOBE BRYANT

CLONE HOME AND AWAY TEAMS

Press C-Up (x7) at the Team Select screen. Then press C-Down the number of times indicated in the code to create a home team. To create an away team, press Z to display the team's statistics before pressing C-Down.

PLAYER	CODE
Kobe Bryant	C-Down (x3)
Ken Griffey Jr.	C-Down (x4)
Random NBA player	C-Down (x5)
Minoru Arakawa (Nintendo)	C-Down (x10)
Tim Bechtel (Nintendo)	C-Down (x11)
Steve Bolender (Nintendo)	C-Down (x12)
John Brandwood (Left Field)	C-Down (x13)
David Bridgham (Nintendo)	C-Down (x14)
Scott Bush (Left Field)	C-Down (x15)
Marc Doyal (Nintendo)	C-Down (x16)
Mike Fukuda (Nintendo)	C-Down (x17)
Jeff Godfrey (Left Field)	C-Down (x18)
Ken Griffey Jr. (Homerun Hero)	C-Down (x19)
Roger Harrison (Nintendo)	C-Down (x20)
Chick Hearn (Lakers announcer)	C-Down (x21)
Robert Hemphill (Left Field)	C-Down (x22)
Jim Holdeman (Nintendo)	C-Down (x23)
Mike Knauer (Left Field)	C-Down (x24)
Kevin Kraus (Nintendo)	C-Down (x25)
Chris Lamb (Left Field)	C-Down (x26)
Michael Lamp (Left Field)	C-Down (x27)
Stu Lantz (Lakers Announcer)	C-Down (x28)
Howard Lincoln (Nintendo)	C-Down (x29)
Ken Lobb (Nintendo)	C-Down (x30)

A B C D E F G H I J K L M N O P Q R S T U V W X Y Z

PLAYER	CODE
James Maxwell (Left Field)	C-Down (x31)
Umrao Mayer (Left Field)	C-Down (x32)
Arnie Myers (Nintendo)	C-Down (x33)
Dan Owsen (Nintendo)	C-Down (x34)
Colin Palmer (Nintendo)	C-Down (x35)
Tom Prata (Nintendo)	C-Down (x36)
Ed Ridgeway (Nintendo)	C-Down (x37)
Henry Sterchi (Nintendo)	C-Down (x38)
Noah Stein (Left Field)	C-Down (x39)
Faran Thomason (Nintendo)	C-Down (x40)
Gail Tilden (Nintendo)	C-Down (x41)
Russell Truelove (Left Field)	C-Down (x42)
Erich Waas (Nintendo)	C-Down (x43)
Phil Watts (Left Field)	C-Down (x44)
Armond Williams (Nintendo)	C-Down (x45)

Hidden Characters.

NINTENDO TEAMS

Highlight Quick Play or Arcade Play, and then press C-Right + A.

CHEAT MODE

At the Main Menu, press C-Up + C-Down to display the Cheat screen. After enabling Cheat Mode, you can enter the following codes:

Cheat Mode.

LONG NECKS

At the Cheat screen, press C-Up
(x2), C-Down, C-Up, C-Down.

Long Necks.

SMALL PLAYERS (AWAY TEAM)

At the Cheat screen, press C-Up, C-Right.

SMALL PLAYERS (HOME TEAM)

At the Cheat screen, press C-Up, C-Down.

SMALL PLAYERS

At the Cheat screen, press C-Up, C-Right, C-Down.

BIG HEADS

At the Cheat screen, press C-Up
(x2), C-Down, C-Right, C-Down.

Big Heads.

BIG HEADS (AWAY TEAM)

At the Cheat screen, press C-Up (x2), C-Down, C-Left, C-Right.

BIG HEADS (HOME TEAM)

At the Cheat screen, press C-Up (x2), C-Down.

A B C D E F G H I J K L M N O P Q R S T U V W X Y Z

NBA SHOWTIME

CHANGE COURT

After selecting your player, press the following button combinations at the Player Select screen to choose your court.

COURT	CODE
Home Team Court	Turbo + Up
Away Team Court	Turbo + Down
Street Court	Turbo + Left
Island Court	Turbo + Right
Midway Court	Shoot + Pass + Up

CHEAT CODES

To enter the following codes, press the Turbo, Shoot, and Pass buttons at the Today's Match-Up screen. Pressing Turbo enters the first number, Shoot enters the second number, and Pass enters the last number. Then press the + Control Pad in the noted direction. For example, to enter the No Hotspots code you would press Turbo (x2), Pass (x1), and then press Up.

EFFECT	CODE
No Hotspots	2 0 1 Up
Show Hotspot	1 0 0 Down
No Player Arrow	3 2 1 Left
Tournament Mode	1 1 1 Down
Show Shot Percentage	0 0 1 Down
Big Head	2 0 0 Right
Tiny Heads	4 4 0 Left
Tiny Players	3 4 5 Left
ABA Ball	2 3 2 Right
Infinite Turbo	4 1 1 Up
Midway Uniform	4 0 1 Right
Team Uniform	4 0 0 Right
Home Uniform	4 1 0 Right
Away Uniform	4 2 0 Right
Alternate Uniform	4 3 0 Right

HIDDEN PLAYERS

To access the following hidden players, you must enter the player's name and pin number:

CHARACTER	CODE
Kerri Hoskins	KERRI 0220
Kerri Hoskins (Alternate Uniform)	KERRI 1111
Lia Montelongo	LIA 0712
Lia in Montelongo (Alternate Uniform)	LIA 1111
Retro Rob	RETRO 1970
Pinto Horse	PINTO 1966
White Horse	HORSE 1966
Small Alien	SMALLS 0856
Large Alien	BIGGY 0958
Nikko the Devil Dog	NIKKO 6666
Old Man	OLDMAN 2001
Crispy the Clown	CRISPY 2084
Pumpkin	JACKO 1031
Wizard	THEWIZ 1136
Referee	THEREF 7777

NBA MASCOTS

MASCOT	CODE
Atlanta Hawks	HAWK 0322
Chicago Bulls	BENNY 0503
Charlotte Hornets	HORNET 1105
Denver Nuggets	ROCKY 0201
Houston Rockets	TURBO 1111
Indiana Pacers	BOOMER 0604
Minnesota Timberwolves	CRUNCH 0503
New Jersey Nets	SLY 6765
Phoenix Suns	GORILA 0314
Seattle Supersonics	SASQUA 7785
Toronto Raptors	RAPTOR 1020
Utah Jazz	BEAR 1228

THE MIDWAY GANG

CHARACTER	CODE
Mark Turmell	TURMEL 0322
Rob Gatson	GATSON 1111
Mark Guidarelli	GUIDO 6765
Dan Thompson	DANIEL 0604
Jeff Johson	JAPPLE 6660
Jason Skiles	JASON 3141
Sal DiVita	SAL 0201
Jennifer Hedrick	JENIFR 3333
Jennifer Hedrick (Alternate Uniform)	JENIFR 1111
Eugene Geer	E GEER 1105
Matt Gilmore	MATT G 1006
Tim Bryant	TIMMYB 3314
Jim Gentile	GENTIL 1228
John Root	ROOT 6000
Jon Hey	JONHEY 8823
Andy Eloff	ELOFF 2181
Mike Lynch	LYNCH 3333
Paulo Garcia	PAULO 0517
Brian LeBaron	GRINCH 0222
Alex Gilliam	LEX 0014
Jim Tianis	DIMI 0619
Dave Grossman	DAVE 1104
Larry Wotman	STRAT 2112
Chris Skrundz	CMSVID 0000
Beth Smukowski	BETHAN 1111
Paul Martin	STENTR 0269
Shawn Liptak	LIPTAK 0114
Isiah Thomas	THOMAS 1111
Tim Kitzrow	TIMK 7785
Willie Morris	WIL 0101
Greg Cutler	CUTLER 1111
Chad Edmunds	CHAD 0628
Tim Moran	TIMCRP 6666

THE NEW TETRIS

KALEIDOSCOPE

In the Audio Options, select Haluci as the song. Then enter **HALUCI** as a name in 1P Mode. To disable the kaleidoscope, you must reset your machine.

Kaleidoscope.

BLOCKS FALL FASTER

In 1P Mode, enter **2FAST4U** as a name.

Blocks Fall Faster.

CPU BLOCKS FALL FASTER

In 1P Mode, enter **AI2EZ4U?** as a name.

ERASE DATA (LINE TOTALS AND RESET WONDERS)

In 1P Mode, enter **01DERS** as a name.

ERASE DATA AND HIGH SCORES

In 1P Mode, enter **1N175R4M** as a name.

A
B
C
D
E
F
G
H
I
J
K
L
M
N
O
P
Q
R
S
T
U
V
W
X
Y
Z

NFL BLITZ 2001

VS CHEATS

You must enter the following codes at the Versus screen by pressing the Turbo, Jump, and Pass buttons. For example, to get Infinite Turbo press Turbo (x5), Jump (x1), Pass (x4), and then press Up.

EFFECT	CODE
Infinite Turbo	5 1 4 Up
Fast Turbo Running	0 3 2 Left
Power-Up Offense	3 1 2 Up
Power-Up Defense	4 2 1 Up
Power-Up Teammates	2 3 3 Up
Power-Up Blockers	3 1 2 Left
Super Blitzing	0 4 5 Up
Super Field Goals	1 2 3 Left
No Interceptions	3 4 4 Up
No Random Fumbles	4 2 3 Down
No First Downs	2 1 0 Up
No Punting	1 5 1 Up
Out-Of-Bounds On	2 1 1 Left
Fast Passes	2 5 0 Left
Late Hits	0 1 0 Up
Show Field Goal %	0 0 1 Down
Hide Receiver Name	1 0 2 Right
Invisibility	4 3 3 Up
Big Football	0 5 0 Right
Big Head	2 0 0 Right
Huge Head	0 4 0 Up
No Head	3 2 1 Left
Headless Team	1 2 3 Right
Team Big Heads	2 0 3 Right
No Play Selection	1 1 5 Left
Show More Field	0 2 1 Right
No Cpu Assistance	0 1 2 Down

EFFECT	CODE
Power-Up Speed	4 0 4 Left
Hyper Blitz	5 5 5 Up
Smart Cpu Opponents	3 1 4 Down
Weather: Clear	2 1 2 Left
Weather: Snow	5 2 5 Down

PAPERBOY

In the Options, select Secret Codes and then enter the following:

EFFECT	CODE
Cartoon Sounds	THUNK
No Time Limit	UNTIMED
Giant Newspaper	SUNDAY

Giant Newspaper.

Invincibility	INVINC
Near-sighted	MAGOO

Near-sighted.

EFFECT	CODE
Invisible Objects	JUMBLE
Random Paper Tossing	RANDOM
Turbo	GOFAST
Screaming Obstacles	SCREAM
See All Headlines	HEADLINE

See All Headlines.

Level Complete	
(Max Subscriptions)	MAXSUBS
Level Select	OBVIOUS
Slow-Motion Mode	WAKING
Small Paperboy or Papergirl	LITTLE

Small Paperboy or Papergirl.

Super Jump	MOON
Jump Springs	ALLJUMP
Throw Paper in Front	FRONTS
Throw Paper Backwards	BACKWARD
Turbo Mode	RUSH
Unlimited Papers	NOBUNDLE

PERFECT DARK

HIDDEN ITEMS

MISSION	ITEMS	DIRECTIONS
1.1 dataDyne: Defection run	Laptop Gun in Perfect Agent	Let the programmer ahead of Joanna. He opens a locked door by the elevators.
1.1 dataDyne: Defection	Dual Falcon	Dropped by the hel meted guard on the third floor down.
1.2 dataDyne Research: Investigation cache	Double CMP150	Get to the weapons control without being seen. The cache is by the maintenance bot.
1.2 dataDyne Research: Investigation	Proximity Mine	On the floor behind the Isotope room.
1.3 dataDyne Central: Extraction	Grenade & Dragon	Get to the elevator without being seen, then kill the guard around the corner and he'll drop the key card. Use it to enter Cassandra's office. Use the grenade to blow a hole in the wall to get the Dragon.
1.3 dataDyne Central: Extraction	Dy357 Magnum	Kill the first five guards without being seen, the fifth will drop the Magnum
2 Carrington Villa: Hostage One	Devastator	Shoot crates on helipad.
2 Carrington Villa: Hostage One	Double CMP150	Kill the sniper near the helipadin under 38 seconds.
2 Carrington Villa: Hostage One	Sniper Rifle	In bathroom next to bedroom.
	Perfect	

MISSION	ITEMS	DIRECTIONS
3.1 Chicago: Stealth	BombSpy	Inside dumpster. Use barrels to explode.
3.1 Chicago: Stealth	Double Falcon 2 Scope	In Pond Punk, on bar to the left.
3.2 G5 Building: Reconnaissance	Crossbow	Punch the 2nd cloaked guard.
3.2 G5 Building: Reconnaissance	N-Bomb in Special and Perfect Agent	By the top exit if you exploded the topmost fire escape exit in Mission 3.1.
4.1 Area 51: Infiltration	Double MagSec 4	Dropped by red and white guard near satellite dish.
4.2 Area 51: Rescue	Phoenix	In hidden room over looking hangar (see strategy).
4.2 Area 51: Rescue	Double Falcon 2 (silencer)	Explosive barrel near start.
4.3 Area 51: Escape	Remote Mines	Get Elvis to contain ment area in under 36 seconds.
4.3 Area 51: Escape	Double Falcon 2 (scope)	In the glass lab behind starting point.
5.1 Air Base: Espionage	Double DY357 Magnum	Punch out the NSA agent near the down-sloping elevator.
5.1 Air Base: Espionage	4 Proximity Mines	In the beginning of the mission, at the end of the tunnel on the left ledge.
5.2 Air Force One: Anti-Terrorism Secret Service	Double Cyclone	Knock out the two agents at the base of the stairs below the President's room. Use the Key Cards to open the two closets here.

MISSION	ITEMS	DIRECTIONS
Secret Service		agents at the base of the stairs below the President's room. Use the Key Cards to open the two closets here.
5.3 Crash Site: Confrontation	Proximity Mine	Talk to Elvis by the UFO before completing any objectives.
5.3 Crash Site: Confrontation ???	Double DY357-LX	Disarm Trent.
6.1 Pelagic II: Exploration	Double Falcon 2 (silencer)	Kill the guard four doors from the beginning without triggering an alarm.
6.2 Deep Sea: Nullify Threat	Proximity Mines	Kill the guard to the left in the hallway after the first cloaked guard room.
7 Carrington Institute: Defense	Devastator	Rescue one of the hostages in the infor mation center.
8 Attack Ship: Covert Assault	Double Mauler	Dropped by middle Skedar on bridge.
9 Skedar Ruins: Battle Shrine	Double Phoenix	Destroy two remain ing obelisks with the Devastator.
10 Mr. Blonde's Revenge	Double CMP150	Dropped by female guard in a room before lab elevator.
11 Maian SOS	Double DY357-LX	Dropped by guard in containment lab.
11 Maian SOS	Psychosis Gun	On table near the start.

A B C D E F G H I J K L M N O P Q R S T U V W X Y Z

CHEATS

FUN

CHEAT	MISSION	DIFFICULTY	TIME
DK Mode	Chicago	Any	Complete
Small Jo	G5 Building	Any	Complete
Small Characters	Area 51 Infiltration	Any	Complete
Team Heads Only	Air Base	Any	Complete
Play as Elvis	Area 51 Rescue	Perfect Agent	7:00
Slow Mo Single Player	dataDyne Investigation	Any	Complete

GAMEPLAY

CHEAT	MISSION	DIFFICULTY	TIME
Invincible	Area 51 Escape	Agent	3:50
Cloaking Device*	G5 Building	Agent	0:59
Marquis of Queensbury Rules	dataDyne Defection	Special Agent	1:30
Jo Shield	Deep Sea	Any	Complete
Super Shield	Carrington Institute Defense	Agent	1:12
Enemy Shields	Carrington Institute Defense	Any	Complete
Enemy Rockets	Pelagic II	Any	Complete
Perfect Darkness	Crash Site	Any	Complete

WEAPONS FOR JO IN SOLO

CHEAT	MISSION	DIFFICULTY	TIME
Rocket Launcher	dataDyne Extraction	Any	Complete
Sniper Rifle	Carrington Villa	Any	Complete
Super Dragon	Area 51 Escape	Any	Complete
Laptop Gun	Air Force One	Any	Complete
Phoenix	Attack Ship	Any	Complete
Psychosis Gun	Chicago	Perfect Agent	1:44
Trent's Magnum	Crash Site	Agent	2:50
FarSight	Deep Sea	Perfect Agent	5:13

NINTENDO® 64

CLASSIC WEAPONS FOR JO IN SOLO

CHEAT	MISSION	DIFFICULTY	TIME
PP9i	Carrington Institute Firing Range	Gold	Complete
CC13	Carrington Institute Firing Range	Gold	Complete
KL01313	Carrington Institute Firing Range	Gold	Complete
Kf7 Special	Carrington Institute Firing Range	Gold	Complete
ZZT (9mm)	Carrington Institute Firing Range	Gold	Complete
DMC	Carrington Institute Firing Range	Gold	Complete
AR53	Carrington Institute Firing Range	Gold	Complete
RC-P45	Carrington Institute Firing Range	Gold	Complete

WEAPONS

CHEAT	MISSION	DIFFICULTY	TIME
Classic Sight	dataDyne Defection	Any	Complete
Unlimited Ammo – Laptop Gun	Air Force One	Perfect Agent	2:59
Hurricane Fists*	dataDyne Extraction	Agent	2:03
Unlimited Ammo	Pelagic II	Special Agent	5:50
Unlimited Ammo, No Reloads	Air Base	Special Agent	2:59
X-Ray Scanner	Area 51 Rescue	Any	Complete
R-Tracker/Weapon Cache Location*	Skedar Ruins	Any	Complete
All Guns in Solo*	Skedar Ruins	Perfect Agent	4:07

BUDDIES

CHEAT	MISSION	DIFFICULTY	TIME
Velvet Dark	N/A	Available by Default	N/A
Pugilist	dataDyne Investigation	Special Agent	6:30
Hotshot	Area 51 Infiltration	Special Agent	5:00
Hit and Run	Carrington Villa	Special Agent	2:30
Alien	Attack Ship	Special Agent	5:17

185

*An alternate way to open the cheats marked with an asterisk is to insert the Game Boy Perfect Dark game into a Transfer Pak, connect the Transfer Pak to any controller, then enter and exit the appropriate cheat menu.

SHIELD LOCATIONS

MISSION	LOCATION 1 (AGENT & SPECIAL AGENT)	LOCATION 2 (AGENT ONLY)
1.1 dataDyne Central: Defection	Floor below Cassandra's office.	
	Dropped by a guard in the far left room, facing away from the elevator.	Bottom floor, right of the right elevator.
1.2 dataDyne Research: Investigation	In the glass case, two rooms past the lasers.	On a crate to the right of the "Caution" door leading to the radioactive isotope.
1.3 datadyne Central: Extraction	Unknown.	Room to the left, at the top of the first elevator. (Same room the Laptop Gun is found in Perfect Agent.)
2 Carrington Villa: Hostage One	On a crate, on the heli-pad.	In the bathroom, inside the bedroom, down the first stairs from the main entrance.
3.1 Chicago: Stealth	Under the grate by the taxi.	Bottom of the stair well in Pond Punk.
3.2 G5 Building: Reconnaisssance	Under the stairwell, between the two exit doors.	Corner of landing and wall, just past the second key card door.
4.1 Area 51: Infiltration	Tunnel between minefield and air intercept radar.	In front of the door, by the satellite dish.
4.2 Area 51: Rescue	Room at the top of main tunnel, on table.	Guard patrolling stack of crates at the start. He normally circles them.
4.3 Area 51: Escape	Medical containment closet where Jo meets Jonathan.	Scientist in cryolab on the right, facing hiding place.

MISSION	LOCATION 1 (AGENT & SPECIAL AGENT)	LOCATION 2 (AGENT ONLY)
5.1 Air Base: Espionage	In the safe with the flight plans.	Guard in black, next to diagonal lift.
5.2 Air Force One: Anti-Terrorism	Piano room, behind short partition.	Food service room in aft middle.
5.3 Crash Site: Confrontation	Next to the President's clone, in a cave with a hole in the ceiling.	Small valley directly below Elvis' spaceship
6.1 Pelagic II: Exploration	On a crate under the left rafter/beam in the lift activation room.	Top deck on the cross-shaped grating, off the GPS objective room.
6.2 Deep Sea: Nullify Threat	End of the tunnel to the left of Dr. Caroll's window.	Unknown.
7 Carrington Institute: Defense	Hangar level storage room with two trenches. The shield is in the left trench.	Alcove past the elevator closest to the Training room, upper level.
8 Attack Ship: Covert Assault	Top of the dual lifts in the hangar, turn right, through a door, on a table.	Unknown.
9 Skedar Ruins: Battle Shrine	In front of S-shaped crack in the short tunnel, area past the blown hole alley.	Behind large, fallen pillar, opposite large target pillar.
Mr. Blonde's Revenge	Same as dataDyne Defection.	Unknown.
Maian SOS	Unknown.	Unknown.
WAR!	Unknown.	Unknown.
The Duel	Unknown.	Unknown.

QUAKE 2

TWISTS DEATHMATCH LEVEL

Enter **FVBS LBBB 7VBC 3BGB** as a password.

Twists Deathmatch Level.

ADDITIONAL COLORS

Enter **S3TC 00LC 0L0R S???** as a password.

LOW GRAVITY IN MULTIPLAYER

Enter **S3TL 0WGR V1TY ????** as a password.

UNLIMITED AMMO IN MULTIPLAYER

Enter **S3T1 NF1N 1T3S H0TS** as a password.

PASSWORDS

LEVEL	PASSWORD
2	PGBR VK?B 65BH Y3HD
3	1KLS DN5H 7NBF DWRQ
4	2KLR SDRY ?VV4 YQ8X
5	VK3T 7LFC 94B7 D3R3
6	WK3H QNBW NLV5 XGL3
7	TK7P 6LLP KWGY XD4V
8	ST0N QPX4 2WGY JXTS
9	R??P 7NY4 2WGX 99TX
10	Q??K BBBV NBQ1 7GCV
11	P64? ZM5B ?BM0 5YH6
12	N664 SQ63 XB?K B7LF
13	M682 M7QT 1215 8098
14	L669 H8MD G8XB JNYV
15	K681 X8CL H01K 1PF5
16	J6?0 BT5M NRZ2 QXLL
17	H6?0 XXFW PHV1 77P4
18	G6?9 GYMK RWNK SMSL
19	F6Y3 WXQK CHD0 8K4D

RAINBOW SIX

RECRUIT DIFFICULTY PASSWORDS

LEVEL	PASSWORD
2: Red Wolf	12D1S2Q22MQQ
3: Sun Devil	BJDBC3Q22WQQ
4: Eagle Watch	BZDBSMQZZ!QQ
5: Ghost Dance	CJTCCQQ2FGSQ
6: Fire Walk	K2TK65Q2F4SQ
7: Lion's Den	T2TT68QGF!WQ
8: Deep Magic	5JR5L1QGGGSQ
9: Lone Fox	52T572Q4G4SQ
10: Black Star	VJVVLJQGGWSQ
11: Wild Arrow	VZVVXMQ26!SQ
12: Mystic Tiger	VZRFTMQ2G8SQ

VETERAN DIFFICULTY PASSWORDS

LEVEL	PASSWORD
2: Red Wolf	1ZL1S2RF2MQQ
3: Sun Devil	BJJBC3RF25QQ
4: Eagle Watch	BZJBSMRF28RQ
5: Ghost Dance	CZBCS5RFFMRQ
6: Fire Walk	DJBDCYRFF5RQ
7: Lion's Den	DJDDC6R2FWR8
8: Deep Magic	LZBDS8R2F8RQ
9: Lone Fox	MJB2D1R2G2RQ
10: Black Star	2ZB2T2R2GMQQ
11: Wild Arrow	FJJFD3R2G5RQ
12: Mystic Tiger	FZJFTMR2G8RQ

A
B
C
D
E
F
G
H
I
J
K
L
M
N
O
P
Q
R
S
T
U
V
W
X
Y
Z

ELITE DIFFICULTY PASSWORDS

LEVEL	PASSWORD
2: Red Wolf	1ZB1S2S22M??
3: Sun Devil	BJBBC3S225??
4: Eagle Watch	BZBBSMS22888
5: Ghost Dance	CJDCCQS2F288
6: Fire Walk	CZDCSWS2FMQ8
7: Lion's Den	DJBDCYS2F5??
8: Deep Magic	DZBDS8S2F???
9: Lone Fox	2JB2D1S2G2??
10: Black Star	2ZB2T2S2GM??
11: Wild Arrow	FJDFD3S2G5??
12: Mystic Tiger	FZDFTMS2G888

ROADSTERS

CHEAT CODES

Rename any character to the following. You will hear a voice say "Congratulations" when entered correctly.

EFFECT	CODE
Disable All Cheats	CheatsOff
All Classes	Gimmie ALL
$250,000	fastBUCKS
$1,000,000	EasyMoney
Hovercraft	Skywalker
Large Tires	BigWheels
Miniature Cars	Car Radio
Overhead View	Chopper
High-pitched Commentary	Smurfing
High-Resolution Mode	Extra rez
(Access in Options)	

SAN FRANCISCO RUSH 2049

CHEAT MENU

Press Z + R Button + L Button + C-Up + C-Right at the main menu.

INVINCIBLE

At the Cheat Menu, highlight Invincible and press C-right, L Button, R Button, R Button, L Button. Then, hold C-left + C-down and press Z.

ALL PARTS

At the Cheat Menu, highlight All Parts, hold L Button + R Button and press Z. Release the buttons, press C-Down, C-Up, C-Left, C-Right, hold L Button + R Button and press Z.

BATTLE PAINT SHOP

At the Cheat Menu, highlight Battle Paint Shop and press Z, Z, Z, C-Down, C-Down, C-Down, C-Left, C-Left, C-Left, C-Right, C-Up, C-Left, C-Down.

SUPER SPEED

At the Cheat Menu, highlight Super Speed, press Z, and hold L Button + R Button and press Z. Release the buttons and press C-Down. Hold L Button + R Button and press C-Down. Release and press C-Up, C-Up, C-Up.

SUPER TIRES

At the Cheat Menu, highlight Super Tires and press Z, Z, Z, L Button, R Button, C-Up, C-Up, C-Left, C-Right, C-Down.

BRAKES

At the Cheat Menu, highlight Brakes and press C-Down, C-Down. Hold L Button + R Button and press C-Up. Press C-Up, C-Up. Hold L Button + R Button and press C-Down.

A B C D E F G H I J K L M N O P Q R S T U V W X Y Z

INVISIBLE TRACK

At the Cheat Menu, highlight Invisible Track and press C-Right, C-Right. Hold L Button + R Button and press C-Left. Press C-Left, C-Left, hold L Button + R Button and press C-Right.

INVISIBLE CAR

At the Cheat Menu, highlight Invisible Car and press C-Up, C-Down, C-Left, C-Right, L Button, R Button, Z.

FOG COLOR

At the Cheat Menu, highlight Fog Color, hold C-Up + C-Right and press L Button. Hold C-Down + C-Left and press R Button. Release and press C-Right, C-Left, C-Right, C-Left.

SUPERCROSS 2000

CHEAT SCREEN

At the Select Event screen, press C-Up and enter the following codes:

EFFECT	CODE
Big Bikes	B1GB1K3S
No Crashes	NOCR4SH
Just Bikes	NOR1D3RS
Extra Camera Modes	MOR3C4MS
All Riders Get in Your Way	BLOCKM3
Bigger Dirt Spray	B1GSPR4Y
No More Off-Track	NOOFFTR4CK
No More Reset	SK1PP1NGOK

EFFECT	CODE
Giants on Mini-Bikes	G14NTS
No Heads	H34DL3SS
Adds Hop Button	HOP
Supercross on Mercury	M3RCVRY
Supercross on Venus	V3NVS
Supercross on Moon	MOON
Supercross on Mars	M4RS
Supercross on Jupiter	JVP1T3R
Supercross on Saturn	S4TVRN
Supercross on Uranus	VR4NVS
Supercross on Neptune	N3PTVN3
Supercross on Pluto	PLVTO

TOP GEAR RALLY 2

CHEAT CODES

Enter the following at the title screen:

EFFECT	CODE
Giant Car	R Button, C-Right, R Button, Left, Up
Rubber Cars	C-Up, C-Left, R Button, Up, Left
Huge Tire	C-left, Z, R Button, Down, Down
Wobbly Tires	R Button, C-Right, START, Down, Z
Bouncy Cars	C- Up, C-Left, R Button, Up, Left
Support Van Repairs All Damage	L Button, Z, R Button, L Button, START
Crashing CPU-Controlled Drivers	C-Right, C-Right, Right, Right, Down
Speed Based Aspect Ratio	Z, C-Left, L Button, Up, Right
No Damage	L Button, Z, START, Up, Up
Hi-Res Mode with Memory Expansion	C-Left, C-Left, Left, L Button, L Button
100,000 Sponsor Credits in Support Van	L Button, Z, START, L Button, L Button
Max Championship Points in Support Van	L Button, C-Up, Left, L Button, L Button
Wide View	Z, C-Right, L Button, Up, Right
Narrow Surroundings	Z, C-Right, R Button, Up, Right
Upside-Down	C-Up, Z, START, Up, Down
No Depth	Z, C-Right, R Button, Up, Right
Speed Warp	Z, C-Left, R Button, Up, Right

WINBACK: COVERT OPERATIONS

ALL CHARACTERS IN MULTIPLAYER

Before the demo, press Up, Down, Down, Right (x3), Left (x4). Then press and hold C-Up and press START at the Press Start screen.

SUDDEN DEATH

Before the demo, press C-Left, C-Right, C-Left, C-Right, C-Up, C-Down, C-Up, C-Down. Then press and hold L Button and press START at the Press Start screen.

TRIAL MODE

Before the demo, press Up, Down, Down, Right (x3), Left (x4). Press and hold C-Down and press START at the Press Start screen.

XENA: WARRIOR PRINCESS, THE TALISMAN OF FATE

BIG FEET

During a fight, hold A and press Right (x2), Left (x2), Right, Left, Right, R Button.

BIG HEAD

During a fight, hold A and press Right (x2), Left (x2), Right, Left, Right, Z.

INVISIBLE FIGHTERS

During a fight, hold A and press Right (x2), Left (x2), Right, Left, Right, Strong Kick (x3), Weak Kick, A.

FIGHT GABRIELLE INSTEAD OF HOPE

At the Main Menu, press Right (x2), Left (x2), Right, Left, Right, C-Left (x4).

GREEN NOSE

During a fight, hold A and press Right (x2), Left (x2), Right, Left, Right, Weak Punch (x2), Right.

ONE-HIT KILLS

During a fight, hold A and press Right (x2), Left (x2), Right, Left, Right, Strong Punch (x3), Right.

INVISIBLE OPPONENT

During a fight, hold A and press Right (x2), Left (x2), Right, Left, Right, Strong Kick (x3), Weak Kick, Z.

PLAY AS DESPAIR

At the Main Menu, press Right (x2), Left (x2), Right, Left, Right.

PLAY AS DESPAIR WITH A BUNNY COSTUME

At the Main Menu, press Right (x2), Left (x2), Right, Left, Right, C-Left, C-Up, C-Right, C-Down.

POLYGON FIGHTERS

During a fight, hold A and press Right, Right, Left, Left, Right, Left, Right, Strong Punch (x2).

PURPLE NOSE

During a fight, hold A and press Right (x2), Left (x2), Right, Left, Right, Weak Punch (x2), Z.

RED NOSE

During a fight, hold A and press Right (x2), Left (x2), Right, Left, Right, Weak Punch (x2), A.

SLIPPERY STAGE

During a fight, hold A and press Right (x2), Left (x2), Right, Left, Right, Weak Punch (x3), Weak Kick (x3), A.

SMALLER FIGHTERS

During a fight, hold A and press Right (x2), Left (x2), Right, Left, Weak Punch, Strong Punch, Strong Kick, Weak Kick, A.

SNOW

During a fight, hold A and press Right (x2), Left (x2), Right, Left, Right, Strong Punch (x2), Z.

TAKE LESS DAMAGE

During a fight, hold A and press Right (x2), Left (x2), Right, Left, Right, Strong Punch (x3), Weak Kick (x3), Z.

NO DAMAGE

During a fight, hold A and press Right (x2), Left (x2), Right, Left, Right, Strong Punch (x3), Weak Kick (x3), A.

TITAN QUEST MODE

At the Main Menu, press Right (x2), Left (x2), Right, Left, Right, C-Up, C-Down, C-Up, C-Down.

ABBREV.	WHAT IT MEANS
Left	Left on + Control Pad
Right	Right on + Control Pad
Up	Up on + Control Pad
Down	Down on + Control Pad
Start	Press Start Button
Select	Press Select Button
A	Press A Button
B	Press B Button

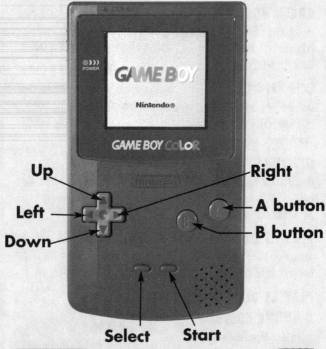

Up

Right

Left

A button

Down

B button

Select

Start

GAME NAME	PAGE
ANTZ	198
ARMORINES: PROJECT S.W.A.R.M.	198
AUSTIN POWERS: OH BEHAVE!	199
AUSTIN POWERS: WELCOME TO MY UNDERGROUND LAIR!	200
AZURE DREAMS	200
BATMAN BEYOND: RETURN OF THE JOKER	200
BATTLE TANX	201

GAME NAME	PAGE
BEATMANIA 2: GACHA MIX	.201
BILLY BOB'S HUNTIN' 'N' FISHIN'	.201
BOARDER ZONE	.201
BUBBLE BOBBLE GBC	.202
BUST-A-MOVE MILLENNIUM	.204
BUZZ LIGHTYEAR OF STAR COMMAND	.204
CARMAGEDDON	.204
CROC	.204
DAVE MIRRA FREESTYLE BMX	.205
DRAGON DANCE	.205
DRIVER	.206
GHOSTS 'N GOBLINS	.206
GODZILLA: THE SERIES	.206
LOONEY TUNES: CARROT CRAZY	.207
LOONEY TUNES: TWOUBLE	.207
MATCHBOX CATERPILLAR CONSTRUCTION ZONE	.207
METAL GEAR SOLID	.208
PERFECT DARK	.208
POWER QUEST	.208
RAMPAGE: UNIVERSAL TOUR	.208
RATS!	.208
REVELATIONS: THE DEMON SLAYER	.211
RUGRATS: TIME TRAVELERS	.212
SAN FRANCISCO RUSH 2049	.212
THE SMURFS' NIGHTMARE	.213
SPIDER-MAN	.213
SPY HUNTER/ MOON PATROL	.213
STAR WARS: EPISODE 1 RACER	.214
STREET FIGHTER ALPHA	.214
TARZAN	.214
TAZMANIAN DEVIL: MUNCHING MADNESS	.215
TEST DRIVE 6	.215
TUROK: RAGE WARS	.215
WACKY RACES	.216
WORMS: ARMAGEDDON	.216
WWF WRESTLEMANIA 2000	.217
YODA STORIES	.219

ANTZ

LEVEL PASSWORDS

02	BCCB
03	DQGH
04	HGGF
05	NBFG
06	KGBF
07	QGJJ
08	GQHG
09	FLDP
10	KGQQ
11	DLGQ
12	CBHG
13	JBJG
14	PLDP
15	LFGB
16	DQLD
17	CLPG
18	DLHD
19	LFQS

ARMORINES: PROJECT S.W.A.R.M.

UNLOCK THE CHEAT MENU

Enter the password, BBBBBBBB to access the Cheat Mode.

ASTEROIDS

CHEAT MENU

During your game, press the Select Button to display the cheat menu and enter the password: CHEATONX

UNLOCK THE EXCALIBUR SHIP

To unlock the Excalibur ship Enter the password: PROJECTX

CLASSIC ASTEROIDS MINI-GAME

To unlock Classic Asteroids enter: QRTREATR

LEVEL PASSWORDS

2	SPACEVAC
3	STARSBRN
4	WORMSIGN
5	INCOMING

AUSTIN POWERS: OH BEHAVE!

HIDDEN MESSAGES

Enter the FAB-DOS emulator and enter in one of the following words to see hidden messages.

SHAG

SHAGADELIC

HORNY

RANDY

BABY

AUSTIN POWERS: WELCOME TO MY UNDERGROUND LAIR!

HIDDEN MESSAGES

Enter the EVIL-DOS emulator and enter one of the following words to view hidden messages.

EVIL

LASER

BIGGLESWORTH

MOJO

AZURE DREAMS

CAPTURE RARE MONSTERS

Use an Ovaseed to capture Guardians and Souvenirs. Throw it at the monsters to catch them.

BATMAN BEYOND: RETURN OF THE JOKER

LEVEL PASSWORDS

2	C76564J
3	L88R8TC
4	Y539WZG
5	NTTJ9KY

BATTLE TANX

LEVEL 3

Enter the password: Green Tank, Red Tank, Blue Tank, Vs

BEATMANIA 2: GACHA MIX

UNLOCK ALL SONGS

Enter the password: YEBISUSAMA

UNLOCK OTHER SONGS

Friends	MELODIOUS
Rydeen	GROOVY
Ultraman's Song	SUPERCOOL
Genom Screams	WONDERFUL
Unknown	SPLENDID

BILLY BOB'S HUNTIN' 'N' FISHIN'

HUNT TURKEY AND PIKE

Enter the password: Pig, Boat, Bag, Deer, Bag, Deer

BOARDER ZONE

BONUS TRACK

Enter the password: 020971

LEVEL 4 & 5 TRICK ATTACK

Enter the password, 290771. Levels 4 and 5 will now be available in Challenge mode.

BUBBLE BOBBLE GBC

LEVEL	PASSWORDS
1	BBBB
2	CBCB
3	DBBD
4	FFBB
5	GGBB
6	HBHB
7	JBBJ
8	KKBB
9	LLBB
10	MBMB
11	NBBN
12	PPBB
13	QQBB
14	RBRB
15	SBBS
16	TTBB
17	CCBB
Boss	VVBB
18	FCCC
19	FDBC
20	GFBC
21	JCCG
22	JBCH
23	LJCC
24	MCKC
25	NCCL
26	PMCC
27	QNCC
28	RCPC
29	SCCQ
30	TRCC
31	VSCC
32	WCTC
33	DBDB

LEVEL	PASSWORDS
34	XBXB
Boss	FCBD
35	GDBD
36	JCDF
37	KGCD
38	LHCD
39	MDJC
40	NCDK
41	PLCD
42	QMCD
43	RDNC
44	SCDP
45	TQCD
46	VRCD
47	WDSC
48	XCDT
49	GBCF
50	HFCC
51	JCFD
52	JBFF
53	KGBF
54	LHBF
55	MFJB
56	NBFK
57	PLBF
58	QMBF
59	RFNB
60	SBFP

BUST-A-MOVE MILLENNIUM

HIDDEN LEVELS

At the main menu press: B, LEFT, RIGHT, B.

BUZZ LIGHTYEAR OF STAR COMMAND

LEVEL PASSWORDS

2	BBVBB
3	CVVBB
4	XBVBB
5	YVVBB
6	GBVBB
7	HVVBB
8	3BVBB
9	4VVBB
10	LBVBB
11	MVVBB
12	7BVBB
13	8VVBB

CARMAGEDDON

UNLOCK ALL CARS AND TRUCKS

Enter the password: OZ6SZD[skull]V

CROC

LEVEL SELECT

Enter the password: PQHPBFDHJB

204

DAVE MIRRA FREESTYLE BMX

FULL GAME

Enter the password: R6KZBS7L1CTQMH

DRAGON DANCE

LEVEL PASSWORD

LEVEL	PASSWORD
1	3128
2	1497
3	7434
4	4136
5	9224
6	6230
7	4592
8	7271
9	2315
10	2042
11	9913
12	9354
13	1720
14	3310
15	0170
16	5108
17	6482
18	1277
19	2460
20	4838

DRIVER

ACCESS THE CHEAT MENU

At the Main Menu screen, enter in the following code to unlock the Cheat Menu.

Highlight "Undercover" and press UP, UP, DOWN, DOWN, UP, DOWN, UP, DOWN, UP, UP, DOWN and DOWN. If you entered the code correctly, the Cheats menu option will become available. Access the Cheats menu and turn ON or OFF any of the options by pressing RIGHT to activate them or pressing LEFT to de-activate them.

GHOSTS 'N GOBLINS

LEVEL PASSWORDS

QUEST 1

Level 2: L Heart K Heart Heart Heart B L

Level 3: Q Zero M Heart Heart Heart 1 H

Level 4: P S 5 Heart 7 Heart B 4

Level 5: T J R Heart 7 Heart 2 Heart

Level 6: J J T Heart 7 Heart 7 L

Final Boss: K D C Heart H Heart S H

QUEST 2

Level 1: G N Heart Heart K O O H

Level 2: G N 1 Heart 5 0 8 J

Level 3: X 4 3 Heart 5 0 M R

Level 4: L S 5 Heart 9 1 1 4

Level 5: D N 7 Heart 9 3 Heart 7

Level 6: X N 9 Heart 9 3 3 3

Final Boss: N 8 C Heart K 4 0 N

GODZILLA: THE SERIES

LEVEL PASSWORDS

02	NCFRGJJBBK
03	DMTFLSBFQM
04	PKDJMPLNPS
05	KDQLHRNDCN
06	DQSPCFPFJR

LOONEY TUNES: CARROT CRAZY

LEVEL PASSWORDS

EASY

01: Treasure Island Marvin Martian, Elmer Fudd, Daffy Duck

02: Crazy Town Daffy Duck, Taz, Elmer Fudd

04: Space Station Yosemite Sam, Daffy Duck, Elmer Fudd

HARD

02: Crazy Town Taz, Marvin Martian, Yosemite Sam

04: Space Station Marvin Martian, Taz, Yosemite Sam

LOONEY TUNES: TWOUBLE

PASSWORDS

Granny's House Pt.1: Dog, Granny, Tweety, Taz, Sylvester

Granny's Cellar Pt.1: Taz, Sylvester, Tweety, Dog, Granny

Garden Pt.1: Sylvester, Tweety, Dog, Taz, Granny

Out in the Streets Pt.1: Dog, Tweety, Taz, Granny, Sylvester

ToyShop Pt.1: Taz, Dog, Tweety, Sylvester, Granny

MATCHBOX CATERPILLAR CONSTRUCTION ZONE

UNLOCK STAGE SELECT

Enter the password, BG6S

METAL GEAR SOLID

NEW OBJECTIVES

Complete the game on EASY to unlock new objectives for the original levels.

UNLOCK SOUND MODE

Beat all the VR missions: Time Attack and Practice Mode.

PERFECT DARK

Use your Gameboy version of Perfect Dark to unlock four cheats on your N64 version of Perfect Dark. Use a Transfer Pak and download your information from the Gameboy version to the N64 version. This will make four cheats available. You'll now have the Cloaking Device, Hurricane Fists, the R-Tracker, and every gun in Solo Mode on the N64 version of Perfect Dark!

POWER QUEST

EASY 999,990

At the password screen enter the password: 1-R-7-5 F-L-V-D F-K-V-C

RAMPAGE: UNIVERSAL TOUR

PASSWORDS

SM14N1230	To play as George
S4VRS4560	To play as Lizzie
NOT3T3210	To play as Ralph

RATS!

PASSWORDS

2	WYH4TFGR9J
3	MMQ1DXXLT5
4	C7CDSFVRTQ
5	CW6F2FBLPG

6	LBBWQVDJJR
7	WRGSCD8QPN
8	BWBK8CBQQ4
9	4XLG-WJRD3
10	M1CS4YNKKW
11	5YMJFYJBC3
12	5TWKTYJCF7
13	CD588DDJ5L
14	BJR9XBLS4Q
15	5VLDPYJ8W?
16	WV4M3FRQKD
17	WDP6PDRM-N
18	VMF7YB9BND
19	BW7Z2CMKS8
20	VXXSTCRBD2
21	W8M-TF1MPX
22	CT3L4DWQ5B
23	MCVRJXPB7W
24	M12?BYFG7H
25	CXCPSFMJ3G
26	VD5H7BRQQ2
27	BWTTZCMM48
28	VWYMTC1NN?
29	V6D61B9SJN
30	BR5GGBMYSG
31	VW1TFC2GX-
32	4TRZ1VQDDK
33	5DYHMXZN5S
34	4Y4J1WZKJ3
35	M6R-DYBNMV
36	5BJDYXZSYS
37	WCY39D2T7P
38	L8NGVWBTJ5
39	MWH2VY4HF1
40	4JC-CVZPBT
41	L1CWSWVMJ5
42	BMJ2BBNTVG

B C D E F G H I J K L M N O P Q R S T U V W X Y Z

43	M-?YSYBCYW
44	W3NBFF2DPJ
45	VQ2C5BJYX7
46	4W1WRW9GXJ
47	B7S??CPKDM
48	C2FBZDPTT4
49	VT?6KC-BLN
50	4ZYT3VRC8X
51	VKLSTCTKNS
52	B4?LJBYCXV
53	W2VCKDTHPJ
54	MSXT4Y5DRB
55	43WCTVRT66
56	WWTK-DKB7-
57	L-1GZVWN?W
58	W9HN5D3CRX
59	M5DKJX5CKW
60	5QJ5FY179J
61	BGJ48CGCXQ
62	LB1?8WSC2M
63	LS84SW2CBG
64	57MWWX6R7X
65	MZ36JXJMM8
66	WXMLTDVNFD
67	WZ?MPD4NRJ
68	BVJDZBZQQG
69	4MZL1WDP86
70	CVNJGDZJW8
71	VNYVYCBSQJ
72	VDFDPCVRQS
73	V5SF1BBL6Y
74	MC256Y2K1H
75	CQFTZFQ75G

REVELATIONS: THE DEMON SLAYER

GET LOKI, PAZUZU AND ASURA

Combine the following:

Suzaku + Kali = Asura (Asura has 1800 hp)
Zenon + Shiva = Pazuzu (Pazuzu has 1720 hp)
Zenon + Jinn = Loki (Loki has 1700 hp)

GET BAAL TO JOIN YOUR TEAM

First beat the game, then play the game again. This time return to Mt. Palo and talk to him. He'll join your team.

GET LUCIFER TO JOIN YOUR TEAM

First beat the game, then play it again, this time, return to the Cave of Oasis. Talk to him and he will join you and your team.

A SECRET CAVE

In Luciferium, walk to the north-west corner. Find the hidden cave by exploring the mountainous region. In the Cave you'll find the Omega Armor, Omega Sword, the Alpha Mail and the Alpha Sword.

GET VAERIAL TO JOIN YOUR TEAM

First Beat the Game. Then Return to the Nest of Zord. Talk to the Monster located on the Former Battleground.

ITEM COMBINATIONS

Lich + Harpy = Kelpie	L15
Mammoth + Kobold = Blue	L12
Blue + Kobold = Kelpie	L15
Kobold + Tanki = Kimalis	L8
Kobold + Kelpie = Larun	L13
Mammoth + Hecket = Kelpie	L15
Blue + Kelpie = Kelpie	L15
Mammoth + Hecket = Gayle	L10
Blue + Hecket = Lich	L1

RUGRATS: TIME TRAVELERS

PASSWORDS

PVCJFJFR	Toy Palace North Wing
BVBYMJLK	Toy Palace East Wing
TPJCKLFS	Toy Palace South Wing

San Francisco Rush 2049

PASSWORDS

TRACK	PASSWORDS
2	MADTOWN
3	FATCITY
4	SFRISCO
5	GASWRKZ
6	SKYWAYZ
7	INDSTRL
8	NEOCHGO
9	RIPTIDE

THE SMURFS' NIGHTMARE

PASSWORDS

02	Brainy, Handy, Shy
03	Astronaut, Shy, Brainy
04	Shy, Baker, Handy

SPIDER-MAN

PASSWORDS

GAME LOCATION	PASSWORD
Venom defeated	GVCBF
Lizard defeated	QVCLF
Lab	G-FGN

SPY HUNTER/ MOON PATROL

UNLIMITED AMMUNITION

At the game selection screen press: UP, DOWN, LEFT, RIGHT, UP, DOWN, LEFT, RIGHT, UYP, LEFT, DOWN, B.

UNLIMITED LIVES

At the game selection screen press: UP, DOWN, LEFT, RIGHT, UP, DOWN, LEFT, RIGHT, UP, LEFT, DOWN, A.

STAR WARS: EPISODE 1 RACER

A FASTER ANAKIN

Collect every racer and Anakin will be able to hit a maximum speed of 735 mph.

TURBO START

As the "1" fades from your screen press the throttle button. If you get the timing right you'll shoot forward ahead of the pack.

STREET FIGHTER ALPHA

INSTANT BISON

During any stage in the game hold A, B and Select until the match starts. Bison will jump out and fight you instead of the regular character.

INSTANT AKUMA

While choosing between MANUAL or AUTO, choose by pressing both the A and B buttons. Hold them down until your match starts. If done correctly Akuma will jump out and fight you.

TARZAN

LEVEL PASSWORDS

LEVEL	COMBO
2-1	4-2-3-4
3-1	1-1-5-6
4-1	2-3-7-4
5-1	7-7-3-1
6-1	6-5-4-7

The numbers above refer to the symbols below.

TAZMANIAN DEVIL: MUNCHING MADNESS

LEVEL PASSWORDS

BLGNGJPDFFTJ	Unlocks China Level
LMBPBKTFKDPK	Unlocks Switzerland Level

TEST DRIVE 6

UNLOCK CARS

Win the Mega Cup and unlock:
BMW V12 LMR

PANOZ ROADSTER

You can select them at the "purchase car" screen.

UNLOCK THE MEGA CUP

Win all of the other tournaments to unlock the Mega Cup.

TUROK: RAGE WARS

ALL WEAPONS

Enter this at the password screen: 5lm2fb

LEVEL PASSWORDS

EASY

LEVEL	PASSWORD
02	K14QF4
03	3T5L31
04	SMJ54M

A B C D E F G H I J K L M N O P Q R S T U V W X Y Z

MEDIUM

LEVEL	PASSWORD
02	3MQTL1
03	Z1KMQ1
04	2TQCMR

HARD

LEVEL	PASSWORD
02	DT5JV1
03	2F5QZM
04	MQ5LRS

WACKY RACES

ALL DRIVERS AND TRACKS

Enter MUTTLEY as a password.

WORMS: ARMAGEDDON

LEVEL PASSWORDS

Jungle	Pink worm, Banana bomb, Skeletal worm, Pink worm
Cheese	Pink worm, Banana bomb, Blue worm, Dynamite
Medical	Skeletal worm, Blue worm, Banana bomb, Banana bomb
Desert	Red worm, Pink worm, Skeletal worm, Blue worm
Tools	Banana bomb, Pink worm, Pink worm, Blue worm
Egypt	Skeletal worm, Pink worm, Red worm, Banana worm
Hell	Pink worm, Blue worm, Red worm, Dynamite
Tree-hut	Red worm, Skeletal worm, Dynamite, Blue worm

Garden	Banana bomb, Red worm, Skeletal worm, Dynamite
Snow	Dynamite, Pink worm, Blue worm, Blue worm
Constyrd	Pink worm, Pink worm, Banana bomb, Banana bomb
Pirate	Dynamite, Blue worm, Dynamite, Skeletal worm
Fruit	Skeletal worm, Red worm, Banana bomb, Skeletal worm
Alien	Dynamite, Blue worm, Red worm, Red worm
Circuit	Red worm, Dynamite, Dynamite, Dynamite
Medieval	Blue worm, Dynamite, Skeletal worm, Blue worm

WWF
WRESTLEMANIA 2000

PASSWORDS

OPPONENT	PASSWORD
Road Dogg	PJH!
Val Venis	PJHT
Jeff Jarrett	PJKB
Shawn Michaels	PJM6
Big Boss Man	PJN9
Ken Shamrock	PJRW
The Big Show	PJSS
Shawn Michaels	PJWZ
Triple-H	PJXC
X-Pac/Ken Shamrock	PJZX
Steve Austin	PJ18
Undertaker	PJ3P
Kane	PJ59
The Rock	PJ7N
Mankind	PJ!C
Kane	PKBY
The Big Show	PKDY

STEVE AUSTIN

OPPONENT	PASSWORD
Ken Shamrock	CSD7
Jeff Jarrett	CSGQ
Road Dogg	CSK8
X-Pac	CSL3
Billy Gunn	CSP6
Val Venis	CSQS
Big Boss Man	CSTP
X-Pac	CSVW
Triple-H	CSX9
Shawn Michaels/Val Venis	CS0T
Big Show	C525
Kane	CS4L
Mankind	CS66
The Rock	CS8K
The Undertaker	CS!9
Mankind	CTCV
Big Boss Man	CTFV

THE ROCK

OPPONENT	PASSWORD
Ken Shamrock	FSDM
Jeff Jarrett	FSH4
Road Dogg	FSKN
X-Pac	FSLH
Mr. Ass	FSPL
Val Venis	FSR6
Big Bossman	FSS3
X-Pac	FSW9
Triple-H	FSXP
Shawn Michaels	FSZ7
Big Show	FS2K
Kane	FS30
Mankind	FS6L
Undertaker	FS7Z
Steve Austin	FS!P
Mankind	FTB8
Big Boss Man	TD8

UNDERTAKER

OPPONENT	PASSWORD
Val Venis	2BDM
Road Dogg	2BH4
X-Pac	2BKN
Billy Gunn	2BLH
Ken Shamrock	2BPL
Big Boss Man	2BRN
Shawn Michaels	2BS3
Billy Gunn	2BW9
Triple-H	2BKP
Kane	2B2K
The Big Show	2B30
Mankind	2B6L
The Rock	2B7Z
Steve Austin	2B!P
Mankind	2CB8
Shawn Michaels	2CD8

YODA STORIES

PASSWORDS

LEVEL	PASSWORD
2	XKJ
3	GJP
4	TDM
5	WTM
6	ZBV
7	QTC
8	TGR
9	VDP
10	BFG
11	FNP
12	STJ
13	FTG
14	BLP
15	YSF

PLAYSTATION 2 LEGAL STUFF

PLAYSTATION LEGAL STUFF

SEGA DREAMCAST LEGAL STUFF

NINTENDO 64 LEGAL STUFF

GAME BOY LEGAL STUFF